Ind

OFF THE BEATEN PATH™

Indiana

OFF <u>THE</u>

BEATEN

PATH™

FOURTH EDITION

PHYLLIS THOMAS

A Voyager Book

The
Globe
Pequot
Press

Old Saybrook, Connecticut

GRM c 1

917.72
Tho

Cover map copyright © DeLorme Mapping
Drawing on page 29 rendered from photograph by Helen K. Link
Illustrations by Carole Drong

Off the Beaten Path is a trademark of The Globe Pequot Press, Inc.

Library of Congress Cataloging-in-Publication Data
Thomas, Phyllis,
    Indiana / Phyllis Thomas. — 4th ed.
      p. cm. — (Off the beaten path series)
    Includes index.
    ISBN 1-56440-517-6
    1. Indiana—Guidebooks.   I. Title.   II. Series: Off the beaten
path series.
F524.3.T47   1995
917.7204'43—dc20   95–13106
                                                      CIP

Manufactured in the United States of America
Fourth Edition/Second Printing

For Gaye —
your friendship has enriched my life
beyond measure

CONTENTS

Hall of Fame Museum, Indianapolis Motor Speedway

INTRODUCTION

Ask almost anyone what images Indiana brings to mind, and—after a long pause—he or she is likely to mention the Indy 500, cornfields, and perhaps the steel mills of Gary. This book has been written to advise you that Indiana offers a lot more than racing, corn, and steel.

State highways and byways lead to some of the finest travel gems in the nation. There are natural wonders and man-made splendors, irreplaceable slices of Americana and futuristic marvels, places stately and sublime, others weird and wacky—a cornucopia of attractions, restaurants, and inns that for the most part lie off the well-trodden paths and are overlooked by major travel guides.

The most difficult part of writing this book was deciding not what to include but what, because of space limitations, to leave out. Therefore, what you will find within these pages is merely a sampling of all that Indiana has to offer. It is my sincere hope that this book will help awaken your sense of adventure and encourage you to seek out other such places on your own.

Indiana's geography is sometimes a bit puzzling to strangers. They are often surprised to learn that South Bend is one of the northernmost cities in the state, while North Vernon is not far from the Ohio River, which forms Indiana's southern boundary. Along the Ohio-Indiana border on the east lies West College Corner, while way down in the southwest corner, just across the Wabash River from Illinois, there's East Mt. Carmel. And the towns of Center, Center Square, and Centerville are about as off-center as you can get.

To further confuse the traveler, a look at the official state road map (available free from the Indiana Department of Transportation, Room N755, 100 North Senate Avenue, Indianapolis 46204-2249; 317-232-5115) reveals four Buena Vistas, three Fairviews, three Georgetowns, three Jamestowns, two Klondykes and one Klondike, three Mechanicsburgs, four Millersburgs, five Mt. Pleasants, three Needmores, and four Salems. Pairs of towns with the same name are too numerous to mention, but would you believe *two* Pumpkin Centers? No wonder the U.S. Postal Service insists on zip codes!

But never mind—this book will at least put you in the right

county. And if you do get lost, you're likely to meet such warm, friendly people along the way that you won't mind it a bit.

If all else fails, you can call the Indiana tourism hotline for help. Dial (800)289–6646 to request free printed materials that will help you plan your itinerary. The toll-free number is answered twenty-four hours a day and is accessible from anywhere in the contiguous United States. You can also write to the Indiana Department of Commerce, Tourism Development Division, One North Capitol Street, Suite 700, Indianapolis 46204–2288; (317)232–8860.

Happy wandering!

The prices, rates, and hours listed in this guidebook were confirmed at press time. We recommend, however, that you call establishments before traveling to obtain current information.

Indiana

OFF THE BEATEN PATH™

Central Indiana

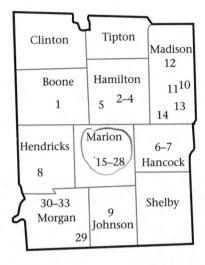

Indianapolis

1. Zionsville Colonial Village
2. Conner Prairie Pioneer Settlement
3. Indiana Transportation Museum
4. Canterbury Arabian Horse Farm
5. Illusions
6. James Whitcomb Riley Birthplace and Museum
7. Old Log Jail Museum
8. Islamic Center of North America
9. Johnson County Museum
10. Camp Chesterfield
11. Mounds State Park
12. Pinebrook Recording Studios, Inc.
13. Alpine Acres
14. The Giant
15. Indianapolis Children's Museum
16. Indianapolis Museum of Art
17. Indianapolis Zoo
18. Eiteljorg Museum of American Indian and Western Art
19. Eagle Creek Park
20. Garfield Park Conservatory
21. Union Station
22. James Whitcomb Riley House
23. Crown Hill Cemetery
24. Indiana State Police Historical Museum
25. Indianapolis Motor Speedway
26. Indianapolis Hall of Fame Museum
27. Ropkey Armor Museum
28. Indiana Medical History Museum
29. Grassyfork Fisheries, Inc.
30. Goeth Link Observatory
31. Link Daffodil Gardens
32. Rock House Inn
33. Boggstown Inn and Cabaret

CENTRAL INDIANA
BOONE COUNTY

The entire community has pitched in to help restore the glory of yesteryear to Zionsville's 125-year-old downtown business district, and its citizens have succeeded admirably. Now known as the ◈ **Zionsville Colonial Village,** it's filled with interesting shops to explore. At Lilly's Boutique Gallery, the selection of unusual apparel and accessories includes many items by more than 125 artists. Three vine-covered buildings filled with a variety of unusual items and nestled in a garden setting are known collectively as Brown's Antiques.

Brick-paved Main Street, which runs through the heart of the village, is decorated with gas lamps and planters. It's here you'll find **Adam's Rib,** often selected as one of the Indianapolis area's ten best restaurants. The adventurous come here to sample the appetizers—such exotic treats as buffalo, llama, giraffe, camel, alligator, zebra, antelope, gnu, lion, kangaroo, and rattlesnake. Not all of this unusual fare is available at all times, so it's best to call ahead if you're yearning for something special. You can, however, enjoy excellent American and continental cuisine any day except Sunday. The prime rib and fresh seafood have been luring customers back for years. Prices are moderate to expensive, and reservations are advisable for dinner. Located at 40 South Main Street, it's open 11:30 A.M. to 2:00 P.M. Tuesday through Friday; 5:30 to 9:00 P.M. Tuesday through Thursday; 5:30 to 9:30 P.M. Friday and Saturday; (317) 873–3301.

For additional information contact the Greater Zionsville Chamber of Commerce, 135 South Elm Street, P.O. Box 148, Zionsville 46077; (317) 873–3836.

The **Boone County Courthouse** in Lebanon, built in the early 1900s, once drew sightseers from around the world. They came to marvel at the eight limestone columns that adorn the north and south entrances. Each gigantic pillar—38 feet high, 4½ feet in diameter, and weighing about 40 tons—is shaped from a single block of limestone.

Lebanon is also the home of Indiana's answer to Willie Wonka's chocolate factory. Any dyed-in-the-wool chocoholic will love a tour of **Donaldson's Country Home Candy Shoppe.** Watch through glass doors as chocolates are cooked in copper kettles and fudge is kneaded on a marble slab. Guides are on hand to explain the history of this favorite confection. Donaldson's produces and sells seventy-five varieties of chocolates, including almond bark, chocolate-covered caramels, hand-dipped creams, and assorted nut clusters. Just when you think you can't stand it another minute, you're given a free sample. The tours won't cost you a cent, and you're certainly under no obligation to buy, but if you don't, you have more willpower than most of us. You'll find Donaldson's at 600 South State Road 39, just south of State Road 39's intersection with I-65 on the south side of Lebanon. Stop by anytime between 9:00 A.M. and 6:00 P.M. Monday through Saturday, but try to avoid November and December; they're understandably very busy months. The management would appreciate it if you could give them at least one day's notice for a guided tour; (317) 482-3334.

Approximately 5 miles north of Thorntown, along U.S. Highway 52, motorists can pause at a pretty roadside stop to eat a picnic lunch and enjoy the pleasant rural panorama. There all similarity to other roadside stops ends, for this is the home of the **Garden of Memories,** a spiritual refuge that is a true labor of love. Reverend Alan Moody, pastor of the nearby Walnut Grove Chapel of Praise, first saw the garden in a vision, and now the vision is well on its way to becoming reality. At present the garden is surrounded by a stone wall that forms the outline of a king's crown. Each of the crown's six points is topped by a glass globe that's lighted all night during summer months and until late in the evening during winter. When you walk through the stone archway in the wall, you're confronted by a rock pile that supports three wooden crosses. There are also winding walkways, a baptismal well, a statue of Christ, and a tiny stone chapel. Eventually Reverend Moody and his interdenominational congregation hope to build a church adjacent to the garden. At the entrance to the roadside rest area a sign reads GARDEN OF MEMORIES—WELCOME! It is altogether a serene and lovely place to be. For additional information call Reverend Moody at (317) 436-7166 or 436-7029.

CLINTON COUNTY

People in Indiana will drive miles for a good catfish dinner—and when they do, chances are they'll be heading for **Miller's Fish**

Suppers in Colfax. A fixture on the Colfax scene since it first opened its doors in October 1946, Miller's occupies an aqua-colored concrete building at 200 West Main Street. The setting is pure Americana—a tiny town, population 800, presided over by a rickety water tower and surrounded by rural countryside. The only anachronism is the mass of humanity that invades Miller's.

Most likely you'll have to take a number, then wander through the crowd outside and find a curb to sit on or a wall to lean against until your number is announced over the loudspeaker system. While you wait, sniff the aroma of catfish wafting through the air, make new friends with other catfish addicts, watch the smiling faces of sated patrons as they waddle out to their cars, note the various makes of cars parked on nearby streets (Cadillacs, Lincolns, and Mercedes are usually mixed in among Fords, Chevrolets, and Volkswagens), and check license plates to see how many states are represented (you'll probably be surprised at just how far some people will come for superlative catfish).

When at last you're seated, you'll find the menu does list other entrées—chicken, shrimp, steak—all of which are quite good. But as proprietors Meikel and Beckie Miller will tell you, the catfish is king. Approximately 85 percent of the meals served are catfish. Once you taste the catfish, fresh from ponds and deep-fried in crunchy corn-meal coating, you'll understand why. Meikel (Mike for short) estimates that he fries approximately 3,000 pounds of catfish a week. Did Mike get into this business because he loves catfish himself? No, he never touches the stuff—turns out he's allergic to fish.

Accompanying the star attraction—three whole catfish per dinner—are French fries, a salad (the homemade coleslaw with sweet-and-sour dressing is recommended), bread right off the shelves of the grocery store, and coffee. But do yourself a favor and order the fried onion rings. If people didn't like Miller's catfish so much, they'd probably come anyway for the onion rings—and maybe for the strawberry shortcake.

Prices are inexpensive to moderate, and the servings are generally humongous. Miller's is open from 4:00 to 10:00 P.M. Tuesday through Saturday; (317) 324–2656.

HAMILTON COUNTY

Bed-and-breakfast accommodations are springing up all across the country these days, and many offer distinctive features, but there's probably only one where you can breakfast with two Siberian tigers. Besides welcoming overnight guests, owner Moselle Schaffer breeds exotic animals on a forty-eight-acre farm named **Camel Lot** near Westfield. The farm is not open to the general public because the insurance costs would be horrendous, but overnighters are welcome to roam the farm at will. Unfortunately the camels that inspired the farm's name are no longer here, but there are llamas, zebras, deer, and tigers.

Guests stay in a private wing of the gray, stone house, which contains a three-room suite complete with four-poster bed, private bath, air-conditioning, and a sitting room in which a camellia tree grows through the ceiling. A full breakfast is served, and if you choose you can enjoy it on a terrace overlooking the pens of the farm's two resident tigers.

Since Ms. Schaffer opened her bed-and-breakfast operation, she has been constantly surprised by its popularity. Her guests have come from all over the world, but her very first customers lived a mile down the road. The second customer stayed three months.

Rates are $80 and up for two. Contact Camel Lot, Ltd., 4512 West 131st Street, Westfield 46074; (317) 873–4370. Westfield is located just west of Noblesville via State Road 32.

◆ **Conner Prairie Pioneer Settlement,** ranked as one of the nation's top five "living museums," will remain 1836 forever. This restored pioneer village breathes life into history, permitting visitors to wander at their leisure through the homes, shops, school, and other buildings that might have made up a pioneer community. "Residents" keep busy at tasks that must be performed to keep the settlement going; they also answer questions about the typical 1836 lifestyle.

Ongoing meticulous research helps ensure the authenticity of the settlement. The orchard, for instance, was first planted in neat rows, but when it was learned that this was a twentieth-century method, fruit trees were scattered about at random. It was also discovered, much to everyone's surprise, that men did not wear beards in 1836, and all whiskers except muttonchops had to go. All lace trim had to be removed from the women's dresses—that was a no-no, too.

Also located on the 250-acre tract is a Federal-style mansion built in 1823 by Indiana statesman William Conner. Visitors can

Conner Prairie Pioneer Settlement

tour the main house and grounds, which feature a springhouse, a still, and a loom house where Conner Prairie staff members duplicate textiles used during the 1830s.

At the Prairie Adventure Center, trained craftspeople are on hand to assist visitors who want to learn pioneer skills firsthand. You can try your hand at such pastimes as weaving on an authentic loom, making candles, and whittling with period tools.

The Museum Center includes a shop that sells items handcrafted by Conner Prairie artisans, a restaurant that features a mix of modern and historic foods, and a bakery that offers nineteenth-century breads, pastries, and cookies.

Special events are also in keeping with the times. Once a month the Methodist circuit rider arrives to preach his sermon. A presidential election is held in the fall, just as it was in 1836. Weddings, too, are authentic, and visitors are often surprised to learn that even in the mid-1800s women did not promise to "obey" their spouses. Brides agreed to "love, honor, and assist" their husbands, who in turn promised to "love, honor, and maintain" their wives.

In 1989 staff members from *U.S. News & World Report* magazine visited the seven most popular living-history sites in the country, Conner Prairie included, and rated them for authenticity and entertainment. Conner Prairie was the only one of the seven to receive the top rating of four stars in both categories.

A program of Earlham College in Richmond, Conner Prairie is located 4 miles south of Noblesville. Open 10:00 A.M. to 5:00 P.M. Tuesday through Saturday and noon to 5:00 P.M. Sunday, May through October; 10:00 A.M. to 5:00 P.M. Wednesday through Saturday and noon to 5:00 P.M. Sunday, April and November; also open at other times for special events; historic areas are closed Easter and Thanksgiving. Admission is charged. Contact Conner Prairie Pioneer Settlement, 13400 Allisonville Road, Fishers 46038-4499; (317) 776–6000 or (800)966–1836.

At the ◆ **Indiana Transportation Museum** in Noblesville, you can follow the development of transportation in America, beginning with covered wagons. There are buggies, automobiles, trucks, fire engines, trains to sit in and climb onto, and a clanging trolley to ride along a 1-mile track. Each weekend a different special event takes place. The museum is in Forest Park, just north of Noblesville at 325 Cicero Road. It's open 10:00 A.M. to 5:00 P.M. Tuesday through Sunday, Memorial Day through the last weekend in September; Saturday and Sunday, April to Memorial Day and October through November; nominal admission fee; (317) 773–6000.

The ◆ **Canterbury Arabian Horse Farm,** also north of Noblesville, welcomes visitors free of charge. You can pet a horse's nose, see a horse "take a shower" in a wash rack, look on as the animals are exercised, stroll through a state-of-the-art barn that rivals horsedom's finest, and, if your timing is right, watch a foal being born. Owners Flois and Debbie Burrow, who acquired their first Arabian in 1980, currently own or board more than fifty horses. Among them is "Real Mac," the mascot of the Indianapolis Colts professional football team. To substantiate the Burrows' claim that they have some of the best Arabians in the country, they point to two bulletin boards covered with show ribbons. The

Burrows' farm is located at 12131 East 196th Street; call (317) 776–0779 before visiting and to obtain exact directions.

If you appreciate cleanliness in the restaurant of your choice, try the **Classic Kitchen** in Noblesville. You can eat off the floor. Not only is the restaurant impeccably clean, but also it serves some of the best food in central Indiana. Its herb bread draws raves from customers, who sometimes opt for additional portions of bread instead of dessert. Not to put down the desserts—discerning diners, who come from miles around, heap accolades on the white chocolate mousse and the homemade key lime ice cream. Prices are moderate to expensive. Open 11:00 A.M. to 2:00 P.M. for lunch and 2:00 to 4:00 P.M. for tea, Tuesday through Saturday; candlelight dinner 6:00 to 9:00 P.M., Friday and Saturday. Located at 610 Hannibal Street; (317) 773–7385.

One restaurant in Carmel takes great pride in fooling its customers. In fact, the hungry folks who flock to ◆ **Illusions** would be disappointed if they *weren't* fooled. Entering via a magical forest that leads to a sword in a stone, they follow directions to open the wall before them and enter a magical world where little (except the food) is what it seems. Menus that mysteriously appear, tableside sleight of hand, and a showroom that features top magicians from around the world are among the pleasures that await diners. Prices are moderate to expensive; reservations are suggested on weeknights and are a must on weekends. Open 5:00 to 9:00 P.M. Monday through Thursday, 5:00 to 10:00 P.M. Friday, and 4:30 to 10:30 P.M. Saturday. Located at 969 Keystone Way; (317) 575–8312.

HANCOCK COUNTY

Hancock County is James Whitcomb Riley country. Here he was born, grew up, and found the inspiration for many of his poems, including such classics as "When the Frost Is on the Punkin," "Little Orphan Annie," "The Raggedy Man," and "The Old Swimmin' Hole."

Riley was born on October 7, 1849, in what is now the kitchen of a white frame house built by his father, who was an able carpenter as well as a lawyer noted for his oratory. Located at 250 West Main Street (U.S. Highway 40) in Greenfield, this house was immortalized in Riley's poems. It contains the rafter room where "the gobble-uns'll git you ef you don't watch out," the dining room "where they et on Sundays," and the side porch where Mary Alice Smith, who worked for the Riley family and is believed to have been the real-life "Little Orphan Annie," would "shoo the chickens off the porch." The ◆ **James Whitcomb Riley Birthplace and Museum,** complete with a collection of Riley memorabilia, is open to the public from 10:00 A.M. to 4:00 P.M. Monday through Saturday and 1:00 to 4:00 P.M. Sunday, April through late December; nominal admission fee; (317) 462–8539.

Although Riley was a lifelong bachelor and never had children of his own, he dearly loved them, and they in turn loved him. The statue of the famous Hoosier poet seen today on the lawn of the Hancock County Courthouse (110 South State Street, Greenfield) was purchased entirely with funds contributed by the schoolchildren of Indiana.

Not far east of the Riley home, at the northwest corner of the intersection of U.S. Highway 40 and Apple Street, you'll find **Riley Memorial Park.** A boulder, into which are carved the words "Riley's Old Swimmin' Hole," stands on the banks of Brandywine Creek within the twenty-acre park and marks the exact spot where Riley and the friends of his youth once whiled away the hours on hot summer days. The youth of today frolic in a modern pool nearby. For additional information contact the Greater Greenfield Chamber of Commerce, 110 South State Street, Greenfield 46140; (317) 462–4188.

Although Riley eventually left Greenfield, he maintained his residence in Indiana until his death in 1916. You'll find his Indianapolis home and burial site described later in this section under Marion County.

Another place of interest in Riley Park is the two-story ◆ **Old Log Jail Museum.** Since log jails could hardly be called escape-proof, their builders resorted to various ingenious methods to keep prisoners incarcerated. This jail features an upstairs cell room and logs filled with nails to prevent prisoners from "sawing out." Nominal admission fee; (317) 462–7780.

If on some warm day you are driving along County Road 300E just north of its intersection with County Road 400N, you may see a kangaroo bounding across the field next to you. Not to worry— you're not entering a time warp, another dimension, or the twilight zone. You're merely passing the **C. C. Irving Wild Game**

Farm, where, in addition to kangaroos, you're just as likely to see camels, peacocks, llamas, zebras, and other exotic wildlife roaming a fenced-in range during warm-weather months. The farm is not open to the public, but the wire fence permits excellent viewing from the road.

At the Irving Materials office, located approximately 5 miles northwest of the farm at the intersection of State Roads 9 and 234 near Eden, you can stop by the lobby any business day to see a collection of rare stuffed animals. Contact Irving Materials, Inc., 8032 North State Road 9, Greenfield 46140; (317) 326–3101 or 634–5802.

HENDRICKS COUNTY

Rising from the cornfields of Hendricks County near Plainfield, the 124-acre ◆ **Islamic Center of North America** has served Muslims throughout the continent as a religious and educational center since 1982. The site, which is the national headquarters for several Islamic organizations, was selected for both its central location and its receptive environment. During the 1991 war with Iraq, the Center's staff members were asked by the Pentagon to advise our military leaders of the religious needs of the several thousand Muslims who serve in the U.S. military. In recent months, the Center also has been flooded with calls from non-Muslims who are interested in learning more about Islam. The public is welcome to tour the mosque, library, and teaching center; contact the Center's public relations department at (317) 839–8157 to arrange a visit. You'll find the Center, distinguished by its modern Middle Eastern design, approximately 3 miles south of Plainfield via Old State Road 267 (Center Street), on the east side of the highway.

JOHNSON COUNTY

The ◆ **Johnson County Museum** is well worth the attention of area history buffs. Housed in a former Masonic Temple, the museum displays more than 20,000 items, including antiques, Indian artifacts, guns, tools, and an interesting collection of nineteenth-century dresses. Four of its rooms have been furnished to depict the period between the Civil War and the turn of the century. But perhaps the most interesting (albeit a bit grisly) exhibit is the blood-spattered fan held by a woman who sat in Abraham Lincoln's box at Ford's Theatre in Washington, D.C., the night he was assassinated.

On the lawn outside the museum is an authentic log cabin built in 1835. It was discovered when an old house elsewhere in the county was being demolished—the house had been built around the cabin.

The museum, located at 135 North Main Street in Franklin, is open 9:00 A.M. to 4:00 P.M. Monday through Friday and 10:00 A.M. to 3:00 P.M. the second Saturday of each month. Free admission; (317) 736–4655.

You'll find numerous restaurants in Greenwood, but one of the finest is the **Johnson County Line,** situated at 1265 North Madison Avenue. Readers of *Indianapolis* magazine recently rated this establishment the "best kept secret" in central Indiana. They loved its prime rib, smoked salmon, steaks, large variety of appetizers, chocolate fondue, homemade cheesecake, and atmosphere. Although the magazine is now defunct, the restaurant isn't. If you'd like to find out for yourself what all the fuss is about, the Johnson County Line restaurant is open 5:00 to 9:00 P.M. Monday through Thursday, 5:00 to 11:00 P.M. Friday and Saturday, and 5:00 to 8:00 P.M. Sunday; (317) 887–0404.

MADISON COUNTY

On the north side of the little country town of Chesterfield, two massive stone gateposts mark the entrance to the beautiful parklike grounds of ◈ **Camp Chesterfield.** They also mark the entrance to another world, for Camp Chesterfield is one of two major headquarters in this country for spiritualists. (For you curious types, the other is at Lily Dale, New York.)

Spiritualists, in case you don't have a dictionary handy, believe that mortals can communicate with the spirits of the dead through a medium. Using a variety of methods, the mediums at Camp Chesterfield attempt to do just that. They conduct seances, go into trances, evoke ectoplasms, cause spirits to materialize, and predict the future. The mediums are carefully screened before being selected to join the camp's staff, and each has his or her own speciality or specialties and sees clients by appointment in

11

one of the cottages scattered about the forty-eight-acre grounds.

Visitors are welcome from 9:00 A.M. to 5:00 P.M. daily and at other times for special events. Fees, quite reasonable, are charged for private consultations with the staff member of your choice, but there is no charge to enter the camp, attend services at the Cathedral in the Woods, view various public demonstrations of psychic phenomena, or tour the fascinating art gallery and museum. The museum houses the memorabilia of the Fox Sisters, who are credited with initiating the modern spiritualism movement.

If you'd like to read up on such subjects as reincarnation, astrology, and faith healing, you'll find books on these and more in the camp's bookstore. A gourmet chef presides over a cafeteria that serves three meals a day, and several hotels offer overnight accommodations. There are even a few campsites for self-contained recreational vehicles. Occasionally you can take courses in such subjects as the technique of spiritual healing, handwriting analysis, and trance development. All rates are reasonable.

Lest you scoff, remember that such notables as Arthur Conan Doyle, creator of Sherlock Holmes, and Thomas Edison dabbled in spiritualism. Even Sigmund Freud expressed an interest in the movement and said, shortly before his death, that if he had his life to live over again he "would concern himself more with these matters." No matter what your beliefs, you will leave here with much food for thought. For a schedule of events and other information, write Camp Chesterfield, P.O. Box 132, Chesterfield 46017; (317) 378–0235. To make hotel reservations write the Hotel Manager at the same address or call (317) 378–0237. The camp is located at the north end of Washington Street in the town of Chesterfield.

Not far southwest of Chesterfield, atop limestone bluffs overlooking White River, you can study the curious architecture of mound-building Indians. Of the eleven prehistoric earthworks preserved at ◆ **Mounds State Park,** the most exceptional is the circular Great Mound (circa 160 B.C.), nearly 1,200 feet in circumference and 9 feet high. Two other mounds are guitar-shaped, yet another is conical, and one is U-shaped. Excavations can be seen, and a naturalist is available to explain the cultures of the Adena and Hopewell Indians, who are believed to have built these mounds. In addition to historical tours, the park offers a swimming pool, hiking and cross-country ski trails, modern campsites, and canoeing on White River. Canoes and ski equipment can be rented in the park. You can reach the park by taking Mounds Road (State Road 232) southwest from Chesterfield for about 2 miles. There's a nominal vehicle admission fee. Write Mounds State Park, 4306 Mounds Road, Anderson 46017; (317) 642–6627.

Gospel singer Sandi Patti, who was chosen female vocalist of the year for eleven consecutive years by the Gospel Music Association, makes her home in Madison County. Her pure, clear voice is captured on albums and tapes at ◈ **Pinebrook Recording Studios, Inc.,** located on State Road 9 in Alexandria. The state-of-the-art facility also produces the recordings of the Gaither Trio and musical scores for television shows and feature-length movies. To make an appointment for a free tour, contact the Anderson/Madison County Visitors & Convention Bureau at 6335 Scatterfield Road, Anderson 46013; (317) 643–5633 or (800) 533–6569.

The Church of God, with world headquarters at Anderson, has established **Anderson University** near the north edge of town. On campus is the ultramodern Warner Auditorium, noted for its architecture. Five days were required to lift into place its rounded roof, one of the largest thin-shelled concrete domes in the world.

Elsewhere on campus, you can visit the Charles E. Wilson Library, which contains the archives and personal papers of the man who served as Secretary of Defense under President Eisenhower. The Wilson Art Gallery houses a $250,000 porcelain bird collection donated by Wilson's daughter and a collection of 1,500 napkin rings that range in variety from a solid gold, jewel-encrusted ring once used by Louis XIV of France to rings made from toilet paper spools in a Japanese prison camp during World War II. More than 10,000 artifacts from the Holy Land are displayed in the Bible Museum, and Reardon Auditorium contains an unusual chandelier that holds some 10,000 light bulbs. During summer months, the National Football League's Indianapolis Colts can be seen practicing on a campus field. For a free schedule contact the Anderson/Madison County Visitors and Convention Bureau (see address and phone numbers in preceding entry). The college is located at the corner of East Fifth Street and College Drive; (317) 641–4233.

At ◈ **Alpine Acres** visitors can watch the fascinating process of handcrafting Bavarian wax from beginning to end. Roberta and

13

Jim Rady, considered masters of this centuries-old art form, started their operation in the garage of their Anderson home in 1982. Since then they've moved their growing business to its present three-acre setting just west of town. The first such operation in Indiana and the second in the country, Alpine Acres remains to this day one of only three places in the United States where molds are made to cast a special wax formula in the same way it is done in the woodcarving areas of Germany and Austria, where the art form was born. Wax art was originally developed because it simulated the appearance of woodcarvings but was more affordable. Today the Radys produce more than 250 varieties of unique collectibles. Free tours are offered by appointment between 10:00 A.M. and 7:00 P.M. Monday through Saturday from April through September and during the first two weeks in December. Alpine Acres is located about 1 mile west of Anderson at 5080 West State Road 32; call (317) 649–4342.

One of the most extraordinary homes in the country belongs to Hoosier musician Vic Cook. Called ◆ **The Giant,** the 7,000-square-foot house overlooks Fall Creek near Pendleton. Its rustic design blends well with the patch of woodland that surrounds it, despite the fact that the house is 254 feet long and soars 38 feet high at its tallest point. Vic Cook is rightfully proud of the ingenious home he designed and built himself from fallen trees on his land, and he is happy to show visitors through it.

The Giant (a name excerpted from "one giant leap for mankind") reflects Cook's philosophy that it's time for people to return to a lifestyle that's in balance with nature. Unlike many others who have espoused a similar philosophy, however, Cook believes we can do so without giving up creature comforts.

Visitors will be amazed to learn that, although his fuel bill is $1.00 a day at the most, Cook's home contains a high-tech recording studio with a fantastic sound system, a big-screen television, two computers, and a washing machine. Perhaps the most unique object in the house is the refrigerator Cook fashioned from a hollow beech tree. Lined with a special insulation, it is cooled by underground air and has a separate freezer section (further cooled by a microchip) that keeps even ice cream solid. Air-conditioning also is provided naturally by underground sources. Cook uses a few kerosene heaters in the winter, but he needs a minimum of fuel because his house is superinsulated. The house is powered by six storage batteries that are charged by solar panels, with a gasoline-powered generator on hand for alternative power when the weather stays cloudy for days. And yes, he does have an indoor toilet—a composting unit.

There's another bonus, too. Because Cook has no utility hookups, his real estate taxes are much lower.

Although The Giant took eight years to build, Cook believes it would be possible for a couple of reasonably fit people to build a similar structure in one summer for about $3,500.

To learn more about the man and The Giant, often described as being at the pinnacle of environmental science, make an appointment for a tour. An admission fee is charged, with proceeds going to a not-for-profit environmental organization. Tours, which include a quarter-mile hike through the woods, are available from April through October. Contact The Giant, c/o EarthShip Corporation, 2928 West Larry Street, Anderson 46013; (317) 778–2757.

MARION COUNTY

If anyone ever compiles a list of national treasures, the ◆ **Indianapolis Children's Museum** should be on it. It is the largest children's museum in the world, and in this case, bigger *is* better. You can ride a turn-of-the-century carousel; explore the twisting passages of a limestone cave; visit a log cabin, an Indian tepee, an igloo, and an Egyptian tomb inhabited by the 3,000-year-old mummy of a princess; stand beside a fifty-five-ton wood-burning locomotive; see a 30-foot-tall glass water clock, the tallest in the world; marvel at an 820-pound yo-yo that actually works (although it has to be lifted by a crane to do so); watch a spectacular collection of toy trains in motion; examine replicas of prehistoric creatures; and conduct scientific experiments. If you can coax the adults away from it, your child can sit behind the wheel of a 1940 Maserati that once competed in the Indy 500. Other exhibits, such as the computer center, provide a bridge to the future. Outer space comes alive at the museum's planetarium, one of the few in the world equipped with a computerized star projector (properly known as Digistar) that simulates three-dimensional flight through space; your children will be even more impressed when they learn that it's the same projector used to create special effects in the *Star Trek* movies. In the innovative Center for Explo-

Indianapolis Children's Museum

ration, designed by teens for teens, young people can develop projects of their own choosing. Playscape offers learning through play for preschoolers while Babyscape provides activities designed especially for children under three. Even the museum's restaurant offers behind-the-scenes involvement—you can stand at a window and watch the bakers make such goodies as croissants and cookies.

The five-level museum nourishes all those qualities we cherish in our children—a sense of wonder, curiosity, imagination, the desire to know and to create, and the ability to dream. And if you don't have a child, come anyway; this is an enchanting place for everyone.

General admission fee; free admission from 5:00 to 8:00 P.M. Thursday, the museum's only evening hours; nominal additional fees for carousel and planetarium at all times. Museum and restaurant hours are 10:00 A.M. to 5:00 P.M. Monday through Saturday and noon to 5:00 P.M. Sunday; closed major winter holidays and Mondays from the day after Labor Day to the week before Memorial Day. The carousel operates from 2:00 to 5:00 P.M. on school days and during regular museum hours other days. The museum is located directly north of downtown Indianapolis, at the corner of Thirtieth and Meridian streets; you can't miss the blue-and-yellow sunrise design of the massive entrance. Call (317) 924–5431 or 924–5437 (the latter is a twenty-four-hour information line).

The ◆ **Indianapolis Museum of Art,** situated on a bluff overlooking White River, is far more than a museum. It's a 152-acre art park that includes a sculpture garden, botanical gardens, patches of woodland, greenhouses, a wildlife refuge, and a fine restaurant. Among its exhibits are the world's largest collection of J. M. W. Turner watercolors and prints outside the United Kingdom, a self-portrait of Rembrandt as a young man, and important collections of Oriental, Chinese, African, and neo-impressionist art. The museum site was once the private estate of Mr. and Mrs. J. K. Lilly, Jr. (of Lilly pharmaceutical fame), and there is also much of architectural interest here. The main exhibition buildings are open, free of charge, 10:00 A.M. to 5:00 P.M. Tuesday through Saturday; open Thursday to 8:30 P.M.; fee for special exhibitions. A donation is requested at the Lilly Pavilion (the original Lilly mansion), which is open 1:00 to 4:00 P.M. Tuesday through Sunday. Many special events and programs are held here. Visitors can purchase a wide variety of flowering bulbs and plants at the greenhouses (open 9:00 A.M. to 5:00 P.M. daily) and used art objects, clothing, and furniture at the Better-Than-New Shop (open noon to 4:00 P.M. Tuesday through Saturday). The museum is located at 1200 West Thirty-eighth Street; (317) 923–1331.

Indianapolis is going wild over its state-of-the-art zoo, a model for zoos of the future that opened to the public in June 1988. Stretching along the west bank of White River, the innovative sixty-four-acre facility is the first zoo ever to be completely designed around the biome concept. Biomes are simulated natural environments in which animals are grouped by habitats rather than by the continents of their origins. Forest animals from around the world, for instance, share the forest biome, while other animals find appropriate homes in the desert, plains, and water biomes. Unlike most of its counterparts, the ◆ **Indianapolis Zoo** combines the best elements of a zoo and an aquarium, with particular emphasis on a marine exhibit that has been called the best of its kind outside of Sea World. The totally enclosed Whale and Dolphin Pavilion, largest in the world, presents animal shows every day of the year, while a vast aquarium offers above- and below-water views of some 200 aquatic species. Only five zoos in the world possess the capabilities to exhibit walruses—this zoo is one of them. Among the things you *won't* find here are cages and bars. Animals and people watch each other across such natural barriers as moats and boulders and, where necessary, through meshwork that disappears as you look at it. One resident giraffe graphically requested a special privilege for his brethren by licking a hole through the wall of the giraffe barn—the barn is now equipped with windows 14 feet above the ground so the lanky creatures can have a home with a view. Open daily 9:00 A.M. to 5:00 P.M. June 1 through Labor Day; 9:00 A.M. to 4:00 P.M. Monday through Friday, 9:00 A.M. to 5:00 P.M. Saturday and Sunday, April through May and the day after Labor Day through October; 9:00 A.M. to 4:00 P.M. daily the rest of year. The zoo is located just west of the downtown area at 1200 West Washington Street; (317) 630–2030 or 630–2001.

Not far away, at 500 West Washington Street, the ◆ **Eiteljorg Museum of American Indian and Western Art** showcases the arts and crafts of the American West in a $14 million building, reminiscent of an Indian pueblo, that's a work of art in itself. Opened in 1989 primarily to house the collection of the Indianapolis businessman and philanthropist for whom it's named, the museum is one of only two of its type east of the Mississippi River. Its still-growing collection, currently valued at more than $45 million, includes sculptures by Charles Russell, bronzes by Frederic Remington, and paintings by Georgia O'Keeffe. Special programs, some especially for children, breathe life into the exhibits; visitors may, for instance, see roping demonstrations or attend a lecture series that offers instructions on how to make a cowboy hat or a lariat. The gift shop features authentic arts and crafts from the southwestern United States. Nominal admission fee; open 10:00 A.M. to 5:00 P.M. Tuesday through Saturday and noon to 5:00 P.M. Sunday; also open Monday in July and August; closed major winter holidays; (317) 636–9378.

The zoo and Eiteljorg Museum lie within 250-acre **White River State Park,** which borders both sides of the waterway for which it is named. To view drawings and a model of what White River State Park is envisioned to become during the next few years and to obtain up-to-date information about planned facilities, stop at the park's visitor center at 801 West Washington Street. Open 8:30 A.M. to 5:00 P.M. Monday through Friday year-round; also noon to 5:00 P.M. Saturday and Sunday during warm-weather months; (317) 634–4567.

One of this copuntry's largest city parks, 5,200-acre ❖ **Eagle Creek Park** is home to bald eagles, coyotes, and deer. An arboretum near the park's nature center boasts a 400-year-old Douglas fir log and a beech tree into which Daniel Boone carved his still-visible initials. (If you wonder why the carving is so high up, naturalists surmise it's because Boone was on horseback when he left his mark there.) Much of the park's summertime appeal centers on 1,300-acre Eagle Creek Reservoir, which features a three-acre swimming beach; pontoon boat cruises; the only internationally sanctioned canoe/kayak regatta course in the country (site of the 1988 U.S. Olympic trials and the 1994 World Rowing Championships); and a marina that rents boats, canoes, and sailboards. Also in the park are hiking, bicycling, and cross-country ski trails; an eighteen-hole golf course; a joggers' outdoor exercise course; a world-class archery field; ice-skating ponds; and sled runs. The park is open dawn to dusk every day of the year; a nominal entrance fee is slightly higher on Saturday and Sunday. Enter the park at 7840 West Fifty-sixth Street; (317) 293–4827.

A marvelous getaway spot, especially in winter, is the serene world within the walls of the ❖ **Garfield Park Conservatory.** Outside, the world may be white with snow, but inside it is summer eternally. Vividly-colored birds live among trees that shade giant ferns and lush vegetation. Tropical fish swim in a series of pools fed by a 15-foot waterfall. Walk beneath the falls and enter the environs of the desert, not barren at all but alive with cacti, succulents, and carnivorous plants. Outside, from May through October, the sunken gardens are brilliant with hundreds of blooms. Garfield Park is located at 2450 South Shelby Street; open daily dawn to dusk; free. The conservatory is open 10:00 A.M. to 5:00 P.M. Tuesday through Saturday and noon to 5:00 P.M. Sunday, with special hours for seasonal shows; free admission except during special shows; (317) 784–3044.

Holliday Park would certainly be a top contender for honors as Indianapolis's most unusual park. Located on the west bank of White River at 6349 Spring Mill Road, the eighty-acre park was initially developed in 1936 as a botanical garden, and the grounds still contain more than 800 species of plants. The park is most noted, however, for its "ruins."

Three stone statues that formerly resided on the now-vanished St. Paul Building in New York City now perch on a ledge atop three Doric columns, dominating a setting that is the focal point of Holliday Park. Three times life-size, the kneeling figures represent white, black, and Asian males who have labored in unity. Just behind the statues is a grotto with a fountain and reflecting pool. Twenty-five 10-foot-tall columns obtained from a local convent when it was razed a few years back surround the grotto and contribute to the ruins effect. Nearby four statues that once stood atop Marion County's old courthouse adorn the lawn. The collection of statuary is not only eye-catching but also an imaginative contribution to the recycling effort. Open daily dawn to dusk; free; (317) 924–9151.

Until 1982 Indianapolis's grand old ◆ **Union Station** stood virtually empty, a decaying monument to the glory days of the railroad. Today, after $50 million worth of painstaking renovation, it is a festival marketplace where people can view architecture restored to its original splendor, shop, eat, enjoy free entertainment, and even stay overnight. More than seventy shops, restaurants, and nightclubs are located here. Among them is The Best of Indiana, which sells James Dean memorabilia, Raggedy Ann and Andy dolls, and "Garfield the Cat" collectibles. (Dean and the creators of the other items are native Hoosiers.) One of the most popular stores, appropriately enough, is the Great Train Store, where railroad enthusiasts will find all kinds of train-related items and souvenirs. Lefties Corner offers gifts designed for the southpaws among us. A 276-room Holiday Inn with a railroad theme occupies a former train shed and features twenty-six suites in vintage Pullman railroad cars. The Union Station complex, located south of Georgia Street, spans 2 city blocks from Capital Avenue on the west to Meridian Street on the east. Union Station is open 10:00 A.M. to 9:00 P.M. Monday through Thursday and some holidays, 10:00 A.M. to 9:00 P.M. Friday and Saturday, and 11:00 A.M. to 6:00 P.M. Sunday, April through September and mid-November through December; 10:00 A.M. to 8:00 P.M. Friday and Saturday, and 11:00

A.M. to 6:00 P.M. Sunday the rest of the year; closed major winter holidays; facility hours vary. Contact Union Station Information, 39 West Jackson Place, Indianapolis 46225; (317) 267–0700 or 1–800–969–1888. Oh yes—you can also catch a train at Union Station. Amtrak provides daily round trips to Chicago; call (317) 263–0550 or (800)872–7245 for schedule and rates.

In the midst of **Lockerbie Square,** a 6-block area of late-nineteenth-century homes near downtown Indianapolis, stands an old brick house once occupied by poet James Whitcomb Riley (for information about Riley's birthplace, see Hancock County earlier in this chapter). Riley spent the last twenty-three years of his life here, and his memorabilia are everywhere. The structure, built in 1872, is recognized as one of the two best Victorian preservations in the country. Nothing here has been restored to the way someone thought it should look—this is history untouched. Riley's pen is on his desk, his suits are in the closet, and his hat is on the bed. The carpets are slightly faded, and the upholstery shows signs of wear, just as it did when Riley lived here. A humble, unpretentious man, Riley would have been astounded to learn that his home is now a major tourist attraction, luring visitors from sixteen countries in a recent two-month period. Located at 528 Lockerbie Street, the ◆ **James Whitcomb Riley House** is open 10:00 A.M. to 4:00 P.M. Tuesday through Saturday and noon to 4:00 P.M. Sunday; closed major holidays; nominal admission fee. For additional information write the James Whitcomb Riley Memorial Association, 50 South Meridian Street, Indianapolis 46204; (317) 631–5885 or 634–4474.

When Riley died in 1916, he was interred in ◆ **Crown Hill Cemetery.** His grave, sheltered by an elegant but simple Greek temple, is at the crest of Strawberry Hill, the highest point in Indianapolis.

Among the other notables buried here are Benjamin Harrison, twenty-third president of the United States; three vice presidents; and the infamous John Dillinger. Ironically, it is Dillinger's grave that commands the most attention. His funeral in 1934 was the only occasion in Crown Hill's history that the cemetery had to close its gates and restrict attendance. Since then it has been necessary to replace his grave marker several times. Souvenir hunters chip away at them relentlessly, and one collector actually carried away an entire tombstone.

Also located here is **Crown Hill National Cemetery**—a

cemetery-within-a-cemetery and the final resting place for nearly 2,000 soldiers, mostly Civil War veterans. The cemetery's main gate at 3402 Boulevard Place is open daily during daylight hours. Before entering, however, you should stop by the office at 700 West Thirty-eighth Street and ask for a map and/or directions to the various grave sites; the cemetery covers more than 500 acres and is crisscrossed by 50 miles of roads. Office open daily 8:00 A.M. to 6:00 P.M. April through September; 8:00 A.M. to 5:00 P.M. rest of year; (317) 925–8231.

Well-traveled deli connoisseurs will tell you that **Shapiro's Delicatessen** in southside Indianapolis is the equal of any in New York or Chicago. Believe them! Shapiro's has been a much-

James Whitcomb Riley House in Lockerbie Square

loved local fixture since 1905, growing through the years and several generations of Shapiros from a small grocery store with a few tables into a deli/restaurant that serves approximately 2,500 devotees each day. You'll find all the usual deli fare here and then some, generously served, moderately priced, and deliciously prepared. The corned beef, made from a family recipe that won a blue ribbon at the 1939 World's Fair in New York City, sells by the ton—about three tons a week, to be exact. Other highly rated treats include matzo ball and vegetable soups, pastrami sandwiches, potato pancakes, liver pâté, pickled herring, and, on Sundays only, *real* mashed potatoes. Don't forget the desserts—food critics and just plain eaters rank them with the best Indianapolis has to offer. The strawberry-topped and chocolate cheesecakes are without peer. Breakfast, lunch, and dinner are served every day of the week (eat in or carry out); open 6:30 A.M. to 9:00 P.M. Located at 808 South Meridian Street; (317) 631–4041. A smaller northside Shapiro's, established during recent years at 2370 West Eighty-sixth Street, is open during the same hours; (317) 872–7255.

It began as one man's dream. That dream became a reality in March 1994 when the ◆ **Indiana State Police Historical Museum** opened its doors to the public. One of only about half a dozen police museums in the country, it was funded entirely by private donations and is filled with exhibits that will fascinate visitors of all ages.

Vintage police cars and motorcycles, an aluminum boat used by state police scuba divers, a copper moonshine still, some John Dillinger memorabilia, handcuffs, firearms, and bulletproof vests are among the artifacts. The Harger Drunkometer displayed here was developed in the 1920s; Indiana state troopers were the first in the nation to use it. Many of the exhibits are designed for hands-on inspection, and children especially love the two-headed police car (which is actually the front halves from two police cars welded together and facing in opposite directions). Kids can climb inside, turn on the lights and siren, and talk on the radio. There's also a tornado room where visitors can learn what to do when a tornado is approaching—no dry facts here but an actual simulated tornado complete with sound and fury.

The museum is the brainchild of now-retired Ernie Alder, the former director of youth services for the Indiana State Police. Located at 8500 East Twenty-first Street, the museum is open 8:00

to 11:00 A.M. and 1:00 to 4:00 P.M. Monday through Friday; also open noon to 4:45 P.M. on the third Saturday of each month from April through October. Admission is free, but donations are appreciated. Group tours and educational programs can be arranged by advance appointment. Call (317) 899–8293.

Just west of Indianapolis is the ❖ **Indianapolis Motor Speedway,** where each May the world-famous Indy 500 auto race is held. When the course is not being used for competition or test purposes, you can see the track as professional racers see it by taking a bus tour around the 2½-mile asphalt oval. Your pace, of course, will be much more leisurely, and you'll learn many interesting facts along the way.

A ❖ **Hall of Fame Museum** inside the track houses a vast collection of racing, classic, and antique passenger cars—including more than thirty past winners of the Indy 500—and some valuable, jewel-encrusted trophies. Perhaps the best-known artifact is the unusual Borg-Warner Trophy, which displays the sculptured, three-dimensional faces of every 500 winner since 1936. You'll also see film clips of old races.

The museum and track, located at 4790 West Sixteenth Street in the suburb of Speedway, are open 9:00 A.M. to 5:00 P.M. daily, year-round, except Christmas. A nominal fee is charged for both the museum and the track tour; tour information and tickets are available at the museum; call (317) 248–6747.

Ever wonder what happens to Indianapolis 500 race cars *after* the race? They sometimes end up for sale at **Chip Gnassi Racing Teams, Inc.,** where recent offerings included a 1990 Lola that once belonged to Eddie Cheever. Estimated to go from 0 to 60 miles per hour in 1½ to 2½ seconds, driven only 4,000 miles, and undamaged except for one minor fender-bender, it carried an asking price of $150,000 (sorry, engine and tires not included, but you do get to keep the decals). A winning race car, such as the one driven by Emerson Fittipaldi in 1989, is a bit pricier, but Gnassi Racing, located at 3821 Industrial Boulevard in Indianapolis, will be happy to work out a deal for you. Call (317) 297–4772.

Indianapolis, which has a well-deserved reputation for being the amateur sports capital of the country, recently became the new home of the **National Track and Field Hall of Fame.** Among the exhibits are a track shoe worn by the legendary Jesse Owens, a hurdle used in 1884, a photographic tribute to Jim

Thorpe, and an unfinished poster publicizing the 1940 Olympics in Tokyo (canceled because of an impending World War II). Located at 200 South Capitol Avenue in the RCA Dome, home of the National Football League's Indianapolis Colts, the Hall of Fame is open 11:00 A.M. to 5:00 P.M. Monday through Saturday and 1:00 to 5:00 P.M. Sunday daily except during some Dome events and on major holidays; hours may be reduced December through February; nominal admission fee; (317) 261–0483 or 262–3406.

Fort Benjamin Harrison has been designated for closure by the Pentagon, but the U.S. Army's huge Financial and Accounting Center, which each month issues nearly $2 billion worth of payroll checks to army personnel around the world, will remain open. Off the front (north) lobby of the sprawling structure that contains the center is the **U.S. Army Finance Corps Museum,** where visitors can see such monetary mementos as World War II prisoner-of-war canteen chits, counterfeit paper money from Korea and the Philippines, financial notes from the Revolutionary War era, and a wide variety of foreign currency. Open 8:00 A.M. to 4:30 P.M. Monday through Friday, except federal holidays; free; (317) 642–2169. It is on the northeast side of Indianapolis. To reach the museum, enter through the fort's west gate, which lies on East Fifty-sixth Street approximately 2 miles east of exit 39 on Interstate 465; follow the signs.

Elsewhere on the base, at 617 Green Avenue, you can browse through the bargains for sale at the **Post Thrift Shop,** a consignment shop that offers used military goods. Along with its inventory of boots, medals, footlockers, and uniforms, the store sells such everyday items as furniture and baby clothes. All proceeds go to a scholarship program for both military and civilian students. Open 9:30 A.M. to 2:00 P.M. Wednesday and Friday, 11:00 A.M. to 5:00 P.M. Thursday, and 9:00 A.M. to 1:00 P.M. the first Saturday of each month; call (317) 547–0151.

The ◆ **Ropkey Armor Museum,** housed in the (big!) front yard of its owner, is the oldest military museum in the state. Owner Fred Ropkey has amassed an incredible collection of war relics that includes the first Patton tank ever produced—serial number 1—and two World War I, horse-drawn, German cannons that once reposed on Monument Circle in downtown Indianapolis. A more recent acquisition is a Soviet-built amphibious artillery piece used by the Iraqi Army during Operation Desert Storm. Other displays in the combination indoor/outdoor museum include military motorcycles, armored personnel carriers, and firearms.

A natural-born collector, Ropkey also invests in antique automobiles, and his is probably the only home in the country that has a NASA Apollo 5 space capsule floating in the family pond.

Occasionally, Ropkey's equipment appears in films or commercials. James Garner drove one of Ropkey's tanks in the movie *Tank,* and another of Ropkey's armored vehicles was seen briefly during a chase scene in *The Blues Brothers.*

The museum, located on the northwest side of Indianapolis, is open free of charge by advance appointment; you will be given instructions on how to get there when you call. Phone (317) 879–1312.

A few miles to the northwest is a shop of a different kind. **N. Theobald,** full of exquisite shapes and forms and shimmering light, will take your breath away. Never has the world *beautiful* seemed more appropriate. Often described as Indianapolis's gift shop without compare, Theobald's is truly one-of-a-kind. Its uniqueness was recognized in 1989 when it received the International Tabletop Retailer of the Year award—an honor equivalent to winning the Oscar. Noted for its collection of Lalique crystal, reputedly the largest such collection in the world, Theobald's also sells the finest of china and silverware to discerning shoppers. Located in the Fashion Mall at Keystone-at-the-Crossing (where Keystone Avenue meets East Eighty-sixth Street on the north side of Indianapolis), Theobald's is open 10:00 A.M. to 8:30 P.M. Monday through Friday, 10:00 A.M. to 6:00 P.M. Saturday, and noon to 5:00 P.M. Sunday; call (317) 844–3927.

The state's first medical center is also the nation's oldest surviving pathology laboratory. Housed in the Old Pathology Building on the grounds of the recently closed Central State Hospital, it remains virtually untouched by time. Now known as the ◆ **Indiana Medical History Museum,** it features a fascinating collection of some 15,000 medical artifacts, including "quack" devices, used in the nineteenth and early twentieth centuries. *Medical Landmarks USA,* a travel guide published by McGraw-Hill in 1990, describes it as a "marvelous museum quite simply without peer in the entire country." Nominal admission fee; open 10:00 A.M. to 4:00 P.M. Wednesday through Saturday, other days and times by appointment. Located at 3045 West Vermont Street in Indianapolis; (317) 635–7329.

Twinkie lovers can watch the spongy treats being made, along with Ding Dongs, doughnuts, and other goodies, at the **Wonder and Hostess Bakery** in Indianapolis. Best of all, the free tours conclude with free samples, coffee or milk, and even some take-home snacks. Located at 2929 North Shadeland Avenue; call (317) 547–9421 for tour hours.

MORGAN COUNTY

At any given time the goldfish population of Martinsville outnumbers the human population about one hundred to one. The goldfish make their home in the spring-fed ponds and tanks of ◆ **Grassyfork Fisheries, Inc.,** which covers 1,500 acres and is one of the largest producers of goldfish in the world. On any given business day a half-million fish, from fantails to the showy shubunkins, are shipped all over the world. Grassyfork is also a major producer of water lilies, and when they blossom on display ponds during warm-weather months, the landscape looks like a Monet painting come to life.

There are no guided tours, but visitors are welcome to view the ponds and observe the sorting and packing operations any business day of the year. Hours are 8:30 to 11:00 A.M. and noon to 4:00 P.M. Monday through Friday and 8:00 to 11:00 A.M. Saturday. The hatchery is located at 2906 East Morgan Street (Old State Road 37 North); (317) 342–4127.

Indiana limestone has been used on a grand scale to build some of the world's most durable and majestic buildings. Since 1970 it has also been used by Martinsville **sculptor Charles Schiefer** to create some much smaller but equally memorable works of art. Schiefer saws, shapes, sands, and polishes his abstract sculptures in a shop adjacent to his country home at 5270 Low Gap Road. Outside, the more than 150 sculptures that populate his ten-acre yard and surround his lake startle passersby and, as the sculptor's fame grows, lure visitors from all over. Most days they find the artist at work in his shop, cutting and shaping his latest creation amid the stone dust that constantly swirls through the air. Schiefer's customers, like his statues, come in all shapes and sizes; they range from municipalities and corporations to homeowners and a group of schoolchildren who raised enough money to purchase a stone rhinoceros they cherished. For additional information call (317) 342–6211.

If you're the type whose curiosity is piqued by life's mysteries, head for Mooresville and nearby **Gravity Hill.** Legend has it that an Indian witch doctor was buried long ago at the foot of this low hill, and the great energy and power he possessed in life still emanates from the good doctor's grave. Anyone who stops his car at the bottom of the hill and puts it in neutral will find himself coasting backward up the slope for nearly a quarter-mile. Don't scoff until you've tried it—witch doctor or no, it really works! Gravity Hill is located on Keller Hill Road, which runs west off State Road 42 on the south side of Mooresville; for exact directions ask local residents or contact the Mooresville Chamber of Commerce, 25 East Main Street (P.O. Box 62), Mooresville 46158; (317) 831–6509.

Astronomers from Indiana University in Bloomington travel to Mooresville to keep an eye on happenings in the universe, for the ◆ **Goethe Link Observatory** is situated there. On certain nights in spring and fall, the general public can share the astronomers' view through the observatory's 36-inch reflector and 10-inch refractor telescopes and hear a lecture that describes current astronomical highlights in laymen's terms. For a schedule, reservations, and free tickets (necessary for admission) write Public Night, Astronomy Department, Swain Hall West, Room 319, Indiana University, Bloomington 47405, or call (812) 855–6911.

Sharing the one-hundred-acre grounds of the Link estate with the observatory are the fifteen-acre ◆ **Link Daffodil Gardens,** resplendent with blooms for about two weeks in late April. The gardens are open daily, free of charge, during daylight hours. Mrs. Link, a nationally recognized authority on the daffodil, raises an array of different types here and is happy to share her garden with visitors. You can call (317) 832–3283 to check blooming times or watch for an announcement in the Indianapolis newspapers. The Link estate, which is at 1660 Observatory Road, lies just off State Road 67 about 5 miles south of Mooresville near the tiny community of Brooklyn; follow observatory signs.

An eye-catching house in Morgantown has for many years been luring architects, geologists, and just plain folks from across the nation. Built between 1894 and 1896 as a private residence, the

Goethe Link Observatory and Link Daffodil Gardens

house is adorned with the turrets, gables, and cones that were popular in the Victorian era, but there any similarity to other houses of its time ends. The walls are constructed of concrete blocks, embedded on the exterior with rocks and geodes of all shapes and sizes, bits of colored glass, seashells, Indian relics, jewelry, marbles, dolls' heads, keys, a boar's skull, and even a picture of two puppies under glass. Since the original owner kept enlarging the house to accommodate a family that eventually included twenty-two children, many of the items on the walls depict seg-

29

ments of family history. Today the fanciful house is a bed-and-breakfast inn that welcomes guests for $50 to $75 a night; rates include a full, all-you-can-eat country breakfast. Many guests schedule a stay on one of the several weekends when "mystery nights"—wherein guests participate as victim or suspects—are held. Contact the ◆ **Rock House Inn,** 380 West Washington Street, Morgantown 46160; (812) 597–5100.

SHELBY COUNTY

An extraordinary dining experience awaits you in Morristown. Nestled amid lovely gardens, the **Kopper Kettle** is as much a museum as a restaurant. It occupies a picturesque, nineteenth-century manor house accented with stained-glass windows and filled with antiques and art objects from around the world. All this beauty should be regarded as a bonus, because the meal awaiting you inside would be unforgettable served in any surroundings.

The wide range of entrées changes somewhat from day to day, but you can't go wrong with fried chicken, steak, or seafood. All side dishes are served family style, and you're encouraged to ask for refills. You won't find anything really fancy here—just plain food distinguished by perfect preparation, moderate prices, and an elegant atmosphere.

Located at 135 West Main Street (U.S. Highway 52), the Kopper Kettle is open for lunch from 11:00 A.M. to 3:00 P.M. Tuesday through Friday. The dinner menu is available from 11:00 A.M. to 8:30 P.M. Tuesday through Friday, 11:00 A.M. to 9:00 P.M. Saturday, and noon to 6:30 P.M. Sunday; closed Monday; winter hours vary. Reservations are recommended; (317) 763–6767.

Tiny Boggstown was until recently just another rural Indiana community—a pleasant place to be but in no way distinctive. In July 1984, however, all that changed. That's when the ◆ **Boggstown Inn & Cabaret** opened for business, and the "joint has been jumping" ever since. At last count, folks from every state in the Union and from more than twenty-five countries (including Russia, Thailand, and Australia) have trekked to the Boggstown Inn for a nostalgic dose of ragtime music. Performers may include piano, banjo, or washboard players; a small band; or singers (a different combination is offered each evening); but the show always features a sing-along. The inn opens for dinner at 6:00

P.M.; the music begins at 7:00 P.M. and continues nonstop until the inn closes at 10:30 P.M. on Wednesday and Thursday and at 11:00 P.M. on Friday and Saturday. Entertainment charges vary, depending on whether you dine there, what time you arrive, and what night you come. Open Wednesday through Saturday, dinner prices range from $10.00 to $16.00 on Friday and Saturday and from $7.00 to $14.00 on Wednesday and Thursday. Reservations are a must and should be made well ahead of your visit (from four to six weeks for the slightly more popular nights of Friday and Saturday). Since few of the roads leading to Boggstown are marked on any map, you'll be sent directions for getting there when you make your reservation. Write the inn at RR 1, Box 38, Boggstown 46110, or call (317) 835–2020. The inn also offers a Sunday brunch to the accompaniment of live piano music; no reservations required (call for hours). During the first week of August, the inn stages a six-night-long **Hoosier Ragtime Festival.**

NORTHEAST INDIANA

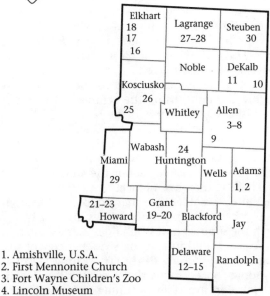

Elkhart 18 17 16	Lagrange 27–28	Steuben 30
Kosciusko 26 25	Noble	DeKalb 11 10
	Whitley	Allen 3–8
Wabash	Huntington 24	9
Miami 29		Wells / Adams 1, 2
Howard 21–23	Grant 19–20	Blackford / Jay
	Delaware 12–15	Randolph

1. Amishville, U.S.A.
2. First Mennonite Church
3. Fort Wayne Children's Zoo
4. Lincoln Museum
5. Foellinger-Freimann Botanical Conservatory
6. Ladeside Rose Garden
7. Cathedral of the Immaculate Conception
8. Seyfert Foods, Inc.
9. Fox Island County Park
10. Auburn-Cord-Duesenberg Museum
11. Ralph Sechler & Son pickle factory
12. Ball State University
13. Ball Museum
14. Muncie Children's Museum
15. Wishon-Harrell Pottery Place
16. Amish Acres
17. Bird's-Eye View Museum
18. Midwest Museum of American Art

19. James Dean Gallery
20. Fairmount Historical Museum
21. Elwood Haynes Museum
22. Highland Park
23. Kokomo Opalescent Glass Company
24. Dan Quayle Center and Museum
25. Lawrence D. Bell Aircraft Museum
26. Warsaw Biblical Gardens
27. Shipshewana Auction and Flea Market
28. Menno-Hof Visitors Center
29. International Circus Hall of Fame
30. Pokagon State Park

NORTHEAST INDIANA
ADAMS COUNTY

Just south of Berne you can drive through a picturesque covered bridge across the Wabash River and leave the twentieth century behind. You are now in the land of the Amish, where windmills replace skyscrapers and horse-drawn buggies move sedately along dusty country roads. This is the home of ✦ **Amishville, U.S.A.,** a 120-acre Amish farm open to the public.

While the members of the resident family go about their daily business of managing the farm, using the century-old methods of their ancestors, visitors stroll through the barn, milk house, smokehouse, washhouse, and old-fashioned garden. Modern conveniences have no place here; the Amish live their lives without motors, plumbing, refrigeration, radios, televisions, and automobiles. At Amishville you can learn all about the simple lifestyle these gentle people have chosen to embrace.

Entrance is free, but nominal fees are charged for a guided tour of the authentic Amish house and outbuildings and for buggy rides and hayrides in the summer and sleigh rides in the winter. In deference to both Amish tradition and the Swiss heritage of surrounding communities, **Der Essen Platz** (The Eating Place) at Amishville serves home-cooked foods that are favorites of both cultures. Two small lakes are available for fishing, swimming, and, in the winter, ice-skating. For those who want to stay a spell and let the peace sink in, there's a large wooded campground.

You can reach Amishville by going south from Berne on U.S. Highway 27 for 3 miles; at County Road 950S, turn east and follow the signs. Open daily from 9:00 A.M. to 5:00 P.M. Monday through Saturday and 1:00 to 5:00 P.M. Sunday; guided tours available daily April through November. Write Amishville, U.S.A., 844 East 900 South, Geneva 46740; (219) 589–3536.

In the Swiss village of Berne, you can visit the ✦ **First Mennonite Church.** Located at 566 West Main Street, the classic Gothic structure is one of the two largest Mennonite churches in North America. Some 2,000 people can be seated in the main sanctuary. Of particular note is the Moeller organ, whose 2,281 pipes have resounded with beautiful music for more than seventy-five years. Visitors come from all over the United States, Canada,

Amishville, U.S.A.

and Europe to tour the church and listen to the organ. The church is open to visitors daily from 9:00 A.M. to 4:30 P.M.; Sunday services are held at 10:00 A.M.; (219) 589–3108.

For information about Berne's unusual shops and stores, many of which cater to the area's 4,000 Amish residents, contact the Berne Chamber of Commerce, 456 Hendricks Street, P.O. Box 85, Berne 46711; (219) 589–8080.

A turn-of-the-century aura of a different sort is found in Decatur. The **Back 40 Junction Restaurant,** famous for both food and decor, is housed in a country railroad station. Outside, on remnant stretches of train track, you can view such railroad memorabilia as a 1920s-era club car, complete with original lighting fixtures, seats, and berths. The "little red caboose" is a gift shop. Inside the station is a fine restaurant decorated with hundreds of antiques and bits of Americana. Antique oil lamps that once belonged to actress Carole Lombard are here, as are a Tiffany chandelier, an old ox yoke, and a collection of the Burma Shave signs that once lined our nation's highways and provided many a laugh. Although the Back 40 Junction offers a regular lunch and dinner menu, it is the moderately priced smorgasbord that has brought it to fame. It's served from 11:00 A.M. to 2:00 P.M. Monday through Saturday, 3:30 to 9:00 P.M. Monday through Thursday, 3:00 to 10:00 P.M. Friday and Saturday, and 11:00 A.M. to 6:00 P.M. Sunday and holidays; closed Christmas. Sing-alongs are a Friday night special. The restaurant is located at 1011 North Thirteenth Street (U.S. Highway 27/33) on the north side of Decatur. Reservations accepted; (219) 724–3355.

ALLEN COUNTY

John Chapman, better known as Johnny Appleseed, traveled on foot through much of the Midwest, planting seeds that would one day grow into vast apple orchards. In his own time he was much beloved, and he remains a folk hero to this day. What most folks don't realize is that Johnny didn't wander about in all those raggedy clothes because he had to. Johnny was a miser—kindly, but a miser nevertheless—who found free room and board with families along the routes he followed, planted some apple seeds in their fields, and eventually moved on. It was no surprise to those who knew him, then, that his death on March 18, 1845, was due to exposure. He died near Fort Wayne and was buried there with honors. His gravesite, open at all times, is located in forty-three-acre **Johnny Appleseed Park,** which lies along East Coliseum Boulevard on the east side of the 4000 block of Parnell Avenue and just north of the St. Joseph River; (219) 483–5532.

The thirty-eight-acre ◆ **Fort Wayne Children's Zoo,** with more than 500 domestic and exotic animals, delights visitors of all ages. Although small, it has been internationally recognized for its landscaping and cleverly designed exhibits. Children love to feed the animals, pet tame deer, and ride the miniature train; the whole family will love the safari through a re-created African veldt where all animals roam free. An exhibit devoted to Australian wildlife—the largest of its kind in North America—includes a 20,000-gallon Great Barrier Reef aquarium. The zoo's newest exhibit, opened in June 1994, is the Indonesian Rain Forest; it features a Sumatran elephant skeleton and an endangered species carousel. Open 9:00 A.M. to 5:00 P.M. Monday through Saturday and 9:00 A.M. to 6:00 P.M. Sunday and holidays, late April through mid-October. Admission fee. Located at 3411 Sherman Boulevard in Fort Wayne's Franke Park; (219) 482–4610.

The world's largest private collection of Abraham Lincoln memorabilia, housed at the ✦ **Lincoln Museum,** includes some 10,000 books in twenty-six languages dealing exclusively with Lincoln; paintings, letters, and personal possessions of the family; and such curios as the flag that draped Lincoln's box at Ford's Theatre. The first item in the collection was the photograph of Lincoln that was used on the $5.00 bill; it was contributed by Robert Todd Lincoln, Lincoln's son, in 1928. A remarkable collection of some 400 pictures of the sixteenth president and his descendants—the existence of these pictures known only to family members for many decades—was acquired by the museum after the death in 1985 of the last of the Lincolns (the president's great-grandson Robert Beckwith). Maps are available for a self-guided tour. The exhibits can be viewed free of charge from 9:00 A.M. to 5:00 P.M. Monday through Friday, 10:00 A.M. to 5:00 P.M. Saturday, and 1:00 to 5:00 P.M. Sunday; closed holidays. Located on the main floor of the Lincoln National Life Insurance building at 1300 South Clinton Street in Fort Wayne; (219) 455–3864. A new gallery, three times the size of the current museum, is scheduled to open in the fall of 1995 at the company's headquarters. It will feature computerized exhibits, film clips about Lincoln's life as depicted in the movies and on television, and additional memorabilia from the collection.

One of the most breathtaking sights in downtown Fort Wayne is the ✦ **Foellinger-Freimann Botanical Conservatory,** a series of three buildings connected by tunnels and one of the largest passive solar structures in the United States. Some 1,300 panels of insulating glass permit the sunshine to enter; moreover, to ensure that all available sunlight could reach the buildings unimpeded, the city passed special zoning laws. Visitors will see displays of North American desert plants, rare tropical plants from around the world, and changing seasonal exhibits. Nominal admission fee. Open 10:00 A.M. to 5:00 P.M. Monday through Saturday and noon to 4:00 P.M. Sunday and holidays; closed Christmas. Located at 1100 South Calhoun Street; (219) 427–1267.

✦ **Lakeside Rose Garden,** which covers more than three acres, is Indiana's only All-America Rose Selection Display Garden. Currently some 220 varieties flourish on nearly 2,500 labeled rosebushes against a backdrop of a lagoon, reflecting pools, and a

Grecian-style pergola. The blooms are glorious from June to mid-October, but the scenic grounds are open daily throughout the year during daylight hours. Free; located in Lakeside City Park at the corner of East Lake Avenue and Forest Park Boulevard; (219) 427–1267.

Anyone interested in architecture will want to see the ◆ **Cathedral of the Immaculate Conception,** a Gothic-style church in the center of Fort Wayne. Its Bavarian stained-glass windows are recognized as the finest in the Western Hemisphere, and its hand-carved wood altar is considered one of the finest woodcarvings in the country. Maps are available for self-guided tours. Open 10:00 A.M. to 2:00 P.M. Wednesday and Friday and noon to 3:00 P.M. the second and fourth Sundays of each month; other times by appointment. Located on Cathedral Square at 1122 South Calhoun Street; (219) 424–1485.

Other notable architectural sights are the **Concordia Theological Seminary** campus buildings designed by Eero Saarinen to resemble an early North European village. They have won numerous national and worldwide awards for both design and landscaping. For a free tour contact the Seminary Relations Department on the campus at 6600 North Clinton Street in Fort Wayne; (219) 481–2100.

The campus of **St. Francis College** boasts a college library housed in a mansion that in the early 1900s was a residential showplace. A stairway that spirals to the third floor of the thirty-three-room Romanesque structure is truly magnificent. A map and self-guided cassette tour describe the lavish wall hangings, hand-painted murals, and period rooms. Located at 2701 Spring Street in Fort Wayne; free admission. Open daily except on school holidays during academic year, but hours vary; (219) 434–3247 (library), 434–3246 (public relations).

Indiana's most honored gourmet restaurant—the **Cafe Johnell** in Fort Wayne—has won front-page recommendations in the *Wall Street Journal* and the *Chicago Tribune,* the *Travel/Holiday* Magazine Award for Dining Distinction (for more than twenty consecutive years), the Mobil Guide Four Star Award (the lone restaurant in Indiana to be so honored), and the Ordre du Merite Agricole from the Republic of France. In 1984 it was the only Indiana restaurant chosen by *Playboy* magazine as one of the country's one hundred finest. With recommendations like that, most anything you select should provide a real taste treat. The cuisine, of course, is decidedly French, and the owners say that among their current selections *sole amandien de Dover, caneton à l'lorange flambé,* and *tournedos de boeuf Rossini* are customer favorites. (Now you have a chance to translate before visiting there.) The chef guarantees that you can cut all steaks with a fork, and the food is complemented by a notable art collection. Dinners range from $30 to $50—prices that are a bit trendy for Indiana but are a bargain in most other places. Open 11:30 A.M. to 2:00 P.M. weekdays, 5:00 to 9:00 P.M. Monday through Thursday, and 5:00 to 10:00 P.M. Friday and Saturday; closed Sunday and major holidays. Reservations are advised. Located at 2529 South Calhoun Street; (219) 456–1939.

While touring Fort Wayne you might want to take advantage of a free potato chip–making lesson. ◆ **Seyfert Foods, Inc.,** goes through nearly 200,000 pounds of potatoes every eight hours, transforming them into potato chips known to aficionados for their extraordinary taste and texture. The secret to the chips' success, say company executives, is twofold—the thickness of the potato slices and the secret-formula cooking oil, neither of which has changed in more than fifty-five years. Seyfert's makes other goodies, too, including cheese-flavored popcorn, corn chips, butter pretzels, and various nut products. Reservations are required for the tours, which are offered at 9:15 A.M. and 1:15 P.M. each Tuesday and Thursday; participants must be age twelve or older. The plant is located at 1001 Paramount Road; call (219) 483–9521.

For a get-away-from-it-all experience, travel southwest from downtown Fort Wayne to ◆ **Fox Island County Park.** There, in a 270-acre state nature preserve, you'll see a 40-foot sand dune and an unusual (for Indiana) quaking bog whose surface ripples when you stamp your feet. Located at 7324 Yohne Road; (219) 747–7846.

The peaceful little town of **Grabill,** northeast of Fort Wayne, is a lovely place to explore crafts and antiques shops. Each year on the weekend following Labor Day, the **Grabill Country Fair** lures people from throughout the Midwest. The fun includes contests for seed spitting, frog jumping, chicken flying, and wife calling. Go north from Fort Wayne onto State Road 1 to Hosler Road in the town of Leo, then turn east onto Hosler Road. For additional information contact the Fort Wayne/Allen County Convention and Visitors Bureau, 1021 South Calhoun Street, Fort Wayne 46802; (219) 424–3700 or (800) 767–7552.

DeKalb County

A rare treat awaits old car buffs in the town of Auburn. Housed in the administration building of the old Auburn Automobile Company is one of the country's finest collections of cars.

The ◆ **Auburn-Cord-Duesenberg Museum** and its contents complement each other perfectly. Constructed in 1930, the building is an architectural masterpiece of the art deco style. The automobiles within it are among the most beautiful ever produced—products of a golden age when luxury and power were the gods of the road. Some 140 classic, antique, special-interest, and one-of-a-kind cars dating from 1898 to the present are on permanent display here.

Indiana was once the automobile capital of the world, and Auburn was its heart, the birthplace of twenty-one of America's early motorcars. The Duesenbergs designed and produced here were the costliest domestic automobiles of the 1920s and 1930s—commanding prices of $15,000 to $20,000 even in the midst of the Great Depression. Greta Garbo owned one, as did Gary Cooper, Clark Gable, and many of the crowned heads of Europe. The cars were not only symbols of extravagant wealth but supremely engineered machines that could hurtle down the highway at speeds up to 130 miles per hour. Today Duesenbergs are worth hundreds of thousands of dollars as collector cars.

Various models of the Cord, more modest than the Duesenberg but still a cut above the rest, and the Auburn are displayed, along with more obscure cars, such as the Locomotive, Rauch-Lang, and McIntyre. A flamboyant 1956 Bentley was owned by the Beatles's John Lennon in the 1960s. Visitors will also see a 1948 Tucker, a car whose history was related in a recent movie of the same name, and a 1981 DeLorean.

The museum is open daily year-round, except for major winter holidays, from 9:00 A.M. to 6:00 P.M. Admission fee; contact the Auburn-Cord-Duesenberg Museum, 1600 South Wayne Street, P.O. Box 271, Auburn 46706; (219) 925–1444.

Each year on Labor Day weekend Auburns, Cords, and Duesenbergs from all regions of the United States return to the city of their creation for an annual festival. A highlight of the event is the collector car auction, which has produced many world-record prices. Even for spectators it's an exciting show. Write the Auburn-

Cord-Duesenberg Festival at the museum's address, or call (219) 925-3600.

In the tiny town of St. Joe, you can tour the ❖ **Ralph Sechler & Son pickle factory,** where multitudes of midwestern cucumbers are transformed into more than fifty kinds of pickles. Along with the traditional types, the factory produces such unique varieties as candied orange strip and raisin crispy pickles. Free tours are offered by appointment from 9:00 to 11:00 A.M. and 12:30 to 2:30 P.M. Monday through Friday, May through October. Located at 5686 State Road 1; (219) 337-5461. A salesroom is on the premises.

DELAWARE COUNTY

In Muncie the winter winds can be fierce, the snows deep, and the temperatures subzero, but in a greenhouse on the campus of ❖ **Ball State University** a tropical garden of orchids blooms all year long. The **Wheeler Orchid Collection** contains more varieties of this exquisite flower than any other collection in the world. More than 7,000 plants thrive here, and the collection's species bank was the first such bank anywhere.

The greenhouse is situated in seventeen-acre **Christy Woods,** a mix of arboretum, flower gardens, research facilities, and nature center that serves as an outdoor laboratory for both Ball State students and the general public. Recorded messages guide visitors along trails that wind through the arboretum (tape recorders are available at the Orchid House). If you come in April or May, you'll also see a profusion of wildflowers. Free; open 8:00 A.M. to 4:00 P.M. Monday through Saturday year-round; 1:00 to 5:00 P.M. Sunday, April through October. Call the Department of Biology at (317) 285-8820 or 285-8839.

The university's art gallery, located in the Fine Arts Building, houses the **Ball/Kraft collection of ancient glass.** Free; open 9:00 A.M. to 4:30 P.M. Monday through Friday and 1:30 to 4:30 P.M. Saturday and Sunday; hours may vary during spring and winter breaks and in the summer; (317) 285-5242.

The name Ball is so prevalent in Muncie because the town is the home of the Ball Corporation, the well-known manufacturer of home canning equipment. In addition to the glass food containers that are the company's specialty, Ball Corporation's plants throughout the world make metal and plastic containers, satellites

41

and space systems, and zinc, plastic, and computer-related products. The ◈ **Ball Museum,** located in the lobby of the company's international headquarters building at 345 South High Street, is open to the public from 8:00 A.M. to 4:00 P.M. Monday through Friday; closed holidays; free; (317) 747–6100.

Although small, the ◈ **Muncie Children's Museum** at 306 South Walnut Plaza has been nationally recognized for the hands-on experience it provides. Children can burrow through a human-size ant farm, learn how to escape from a building "on fire," join a railroad crew laying track across the country, and climb over, under, through, and on ten separate structures. Sunday-afternoon visitors are treated to free "Garfield the Cat" movies (Indiana-born Jim Davis, Garfield's creator, lives near Muncie). Nominal admission fee; open 10:00 A.M. to 5:00 P.M. Tuesday through Saturday and 1:00 to 5:00 P.M. Sunday; closed July 4, Thanksgiving, December 25, and January 1; (317) 286–1660.

Once the pottery handcrafted by Jim Wishon and Jerry Harrell was sold nationwide in such fine department stores as Nieman-Marcus, Gumps, Burdines, and Carson-Pirie-Scott. Nowadays their entire output is sold through their showroom at 1508 West Jackson Street in Muncie. You can watch the whole production process, from shaping on the potter's wheel to final firing at a temperature of 2,350 degrees, in the ◈ **Wishon-Harrell Pottery Place** and then browse through their showroom of finished stoneware. Standard items include wine carafes, pie plates, pitchers, tea sets, mood lights, and dinnerware. Normally open 9:00 A.M. to 5:00 P.M. Tuesday through Saturday; but hours vary, and it's best to check in advance by calling (317) 288–6633.

ELKHART COUNTY

Some of the best farm cooking you'll ever treat your taste buds to is served up at the **Patchwork Quilt Country Inn** in Middlebury. Located on a 260-acre working farm, the dining room is famous for the family-style, all-you-can-eat dinners it serves five nights a week.

When guests arrive they're served seasonal drinks (no alcohol) in the parlor and encouraged to mingle until the dinner bell sounds. No printed menu—your waitress will give you a choice of foods as each course is served. The entrée may be open-hearth baked ham, herb roast beef, burgundy steak, seafood, or butter-milk pecan chicken (the latter once won a $5,000 first prize for the best chicken recipe in the United States). When the dessert tray arrives, you'll find it almost impossible to choose from the luscious-looking treats displayed thereon—if indeed you have enough room left to make any choice at all. You'll be confronted with such unusual meal toppers as cheddar cheesecake, coffee tof-fee pie, Charlotte russe, walnut torte, fruit parfait, grasshopper pie, and candied violet cake—delectable one and all. Probably at least one dessert will feature strawberries—the inn's strawberry recipes too have won national fame.

The Patchwork Quilt also offers overnight bed-and-breakfast accommodations Tuesday through Friday. Three guest bedrooms are available, each with its own handmade patchwork quilt. A deluxe continental breakfast is included in the room rate.

Middlebury is in the heart of one of the largest Amish settle-ments in the country, and the inn offers a guided tour that affords a look at the lifestyle of these people. It also hosts a quilts and crafts tour.

To reach the Patchwork Quilt Inn, go north from Middlebury on State Road 13 for 8 miles to County Road 2, then turn west for about 1 mile to the inn. Lunch is served from 11:00 A.M. to 2:00 P.M., dinner from 4:30 to 8:00 P.M. Tuesday through Saturday. Din-ner guests can choose between family-style and plate dinners. Closed all major holidays and three weeks in January/February (exact dates depend on the weather). Prices are moderate; reserva-tions are recommended at all times and are required for tours and overnight accommodations. Smoking is not allowed anywhere on the premises. Write the Patchwork Quilt Inn, 11748 County Road 2, Middlebury 46540; (219) 825–2417.

You can sample authentic Amish cuisine, as well as good coun-try cooking, in Middlebury. The **Village Inn Restaurant** is a small lunchroom whose customers are as apt to ride up in horse-drawn buggies as in automobiles. All the food is hearty and good—not to mention loaded with calories—but the pies are splendid, the prices quite reasonable, and the people—both staff and guests—delightful. The Village Inn, located at 107 South Main Street, is open from 5:00 A.M. to 9:00 P.M. Monday through Satur-day; (219) 825–2043.

Three miles east of Middlebury at 11275 County Road 250N,

you can tour the **Deutsch Kase Haus** and watch Amish cheese-makers at work. The free samples in the gift shop will help you choose your favorite flavor. Open 8:00 A.M. to 5:00 P.M. Monday through Friday and 8:00 A.M. to 3:00 P.M. Saturday; phone at (219) 825–9511 for the cheese-making schedule.

The area in which Middlebury lies, known as the Crystal Valley, is chock-full of fascinating places to explore and enjoy—quilt shops, antiques shops, country stores, craft shops, furniture stores, and restaurants. For a map of the area and additional information, write the Crystal Valley Tourist Association, 426 North Main Street, P.O. Box 55, Middlebury 46540; (219) 825–5413.

One of the best ways to gain insight into the lifestyle of the Amish is through a visit to ◆ **Amish Acres,** an authentic eighty-acre restoration of a century-old farming community in Nappanee. Amish farmhouses dot the countryside, flat-topped black buggies wander the roads, farmers plow the fields, livestock graze behind split-rail fences, and women quilt, bake in an outdoor oven, and dip candles. You can see demonstrations of soap making, horseshoeing, and meat preserving and visit a bakery, a meat and cheese shop, an antique soda fountain and fudgery, a cider mill, a smokehouse, a mint still, and a sawmill. For the 2,000 Old Order Amish who live in this area, life goes on as it did a hundred years ago.

You may want to take a horse-drawn buggy ride or enjoy the excellent Amish cooking at the Restaurant Barn. The soup is always on in big iron kettles, and such typical dishes as noodles, spiced apples, sweet-and-sour cabbage salad, and shoofly pie are on the menu.

Amish Acres is located on U.S. Highway 6, 1 mile west of Nappanee. The restored farm is open 7:00 A.M. to 8:00 P.M. Monday through Saturday and 11:00 A.M. to 6:00 P.M. Sunday, May through October; tours, rides, and some shops close at 5:00 P.M. Closed Sunday from November through April. The restaurant is open 7:00 A.M. to 8:00 P.M. Monday through Saturday and 7:00 A.M. to 6:00 P.M. Sunday, February through December. Admission fee; special package price for a guided tour. Write the Amish Acres Visitor Information Center, 1600 West Market Street, Nappanee 46550; (219) 773–4188. The information center also can assist you in making reservations for an overnight stay in an area farm home.

Like the Crystal Valley to the northeast, the area in and around Nappanee abounds with interesting shops and Amish businesses that can be toured. The Nappanee Chamber of Commerce, at 215 West Market Street, Nappanee 46550, will be happy to provide you with additional information; (219) 773–7812.

Directly north of Nappanee via State Road 19 is the village of Wakarusa, where you can visit the unusual ◆ **Bird's-Eye View Museum.** Area buildings of distinctive architectural style are reconstructed from toothpicks, popsicle sticks, and other pint-size materials—all built on the same scale (1 inch equals 5 feet). The project began when Devon Rose built a miniature feed mill for his son's electric-train layout and continued until the town of Wakarusa had been replicated in the most minute detail. Now one of the largest collections of miniatures in the world, it has won several awards. Located at 325 South Elkhart Street, the museum is open 8:00 A.M. to 5:00 P.M. Monday through Friday and 8:00 A.M. to noon Saturday. Nominal admission fee; (219) 862–2367.

The ◆ **Midwest Museum of American Art** would be a gem anywhere, but in the small municipality of Elkhart (population 43,000) it is a crown jewel. Noted for its extensive collections of Norman Rockwell lithographs (believed to be the largest collection anywhere) and photographs by such distinguished photographers as Ansel Adams, the museum has become one of Indiana's most important art institutions. Nominal admission fee; open 11:00 A.M. to 5:00 P.M. Tuesday through Friday and 1:00 to 4:00 P.M. Saturday and Sunday. Open free of charge 7:00 to 9:00 P.M. Thursday. Located at 429 South Main Street; (219) 293–6660.

GRANT COUNTY

The death of James Dean on September 30, 1955, catapulted the popular young actor to enduring fame as a cult hero. Although he made only three movies—*East of Eden, Rebel Without a Cause,* and *Giant*—Dean gave voice through his roles to the restlessness and discontent of his generation. He died at age twenty-four, the victim of a one-car accident on a California highway moments after he had been given a speeding ticket, and his family brought him home to Indiana to bury him. Today rarely a day goes by—no matter what the weather—that someone doesn't show up in **Park**

Cemetery at Fairmount, where Dean grew up, to see his grave and mourn his passing.

For ten years after his death, Warner Brothers received as many as 7,000 letters a month addressed to Dean from devoted fans who refused to accept his death. His tombstone in Park Cemetery, defaced by souvenir seekers, was replaced in 1985. Within a few short months it, too, was defaced. A sign that read THIS WAY TO JAMES DEAN'S GRAVE lasted one afternoon, and handfuls of dirt regularly disappear from his burial site. People from as far away as Germany have wanted to purchase a plot here so they can "be buried near Jimmy." It is a phenomenon that shows no signs of letting up and can never be fully explained—a charisma that reaches out even from the grave. Park Cemetery, open daily dawn to dusk, is on County Road 150E; (317) 948–4040.

At the ◆ **James Dean Gallery** in Fairmount, exhibits from more than twenty different countries constitute the world's largest collection of Dean memorabilia. Visitors will see such items as a rare Warner Brothers life mask, original movie posters, clothing from the actor's films, and yearbooks from Fairmount High School, which counted Dean among its 1949 graduates. It won't surprise basketball-crazy Hoosiers (others, maybe, but not Hoosiers) to learn that some folks hereabouts remember Dean first as the clutch-shooting guard of the local high school basketball team and a distant second as a movie star. Located at 425 North Main Street; nominal admission fee. Open 10:00 A.M. to 5:00 P.M. daily; (317) 948–3326.

The ◆ **Fairmount Historical Museum** at 203 East Washington Street tells the story of Dean's life through a series of exhibits and a display of some of Dean's possessions from a family collection. Each September, near the date of Dean's death, the museum hosts the Fairmount Museum Days and the James Dean Film Festival. The museum also honors Fairmount's other favorite son—Jim Davis, creator of "Garfield the Cat." No admission fee, but donations are accepted. Open 10:00 A.M. to 5:00 P.M. Monday through Saturday and noon to 5:00 P.M. Sunday, March through November; also open on February 8 (Dean's birth date), September 30 (the anniversary of his death), and by appointment. Write Fairmount Historical Museum, Box 92, Fairmount 46928; (317) 948–4555 or 948–4776.

The nearby town of Marion, where James Dean was born, is

46

Fairmount Historical Museum

noted for its extraordinary **Easter pageant,** presented each Easter morning at 6:00 A.M. Lauded as the equal of Oberammergau's famous passion play, the pageant draws spectators from all fifty states and from overseas. Free; for tickets and information contact the Marion Indiana Easter Pageant, Inc., 118 North Washington Street, Marion 46952; (317) 664–3947.

Ice-cream lovers will want to journey over to Upland, home of Taylor University, and visit **Ivanhoe's.** When they spy the menu here, they'll think they've died and gone to heaven. Sundae and shake flavors are arranged alphabetically—one hundred delicious flavors each, plus a special section for extras. Hoe's, as it's known locally, also serves ice-cream sodas, floats, and excellent sandwiches and salads. Located at 914 South Main Street, it's open from 11:00 A.M. to 10:00 P.M. Monday through Thursday, 11:00 A.M. to 11:00 P.M. Friday and Saturday, and 2:00 to 10:00 P.M. Sunday. Call (317) 998–7261.

HOWARD COUNTY

The world has stainless steel because Kokomo inventor Elwood Haynes wanted to please his wife. Well aware of her husband's ingenuity, Mrs. Haynes asked him to perfect some tarnish-free dinnerware for her. And in 1912 he did.

The remarkable Mr. Haynes also invented the first successful commercial automobile. On July 4, 1894, he put his gasoline-powered creation to the test on Pumpkinvine Pike east of Kokomo, speeding along at 7 miles per hour for a distance of about 6 miles. That same car is now on display at the Smithsonian Institution in Washington, D.C.

Another of Haynes's inventions is stellite, an alloy used today in spacecraft jet engines, dental instruments, and nuclear power plants. New uses are still being found for it.

The ◆ **Elwood Haynes Museum,** housed in Haynes's former residence, contains a vast collection of Haynes's personal possessions and his many inventions. Visitors particularly enjoy the 1905 Haynes automobile, in which the driver sits in the backseat. Other exhibits reflect Howard County's history during and after the area's great gas boom.

The largest natural gas gusher ever brought into production in this country was struck in 1887 in what is now southeast Kokomo. Almost overnight the town was transformed into a center of industry. Kokomo's many contributions to the industrial growth of America, in addition to Haynes's inventions, have earned it the nickname "City of Firsts." Among the items first produced here were the pneumatic rubber tire, the carburetor, the mechanical corn picker, canned tomato juice, and the all-transistor car radio. These items and more are featured in the upstairs rooms of the Elwood Haynes Museum, located at 1915 South Webster Street. Free of charge, it's open 1:00 to 4:00 P.M. Tuesday through Saturday and 1:00 to 5:00 P.M. Sunday; closed Monday and holidays; (317) 452–3471.

Just to the northwest of the Haynes Museum, at 902 West Deffenbaugh Street, enter ◆ **Highland Park** and view Kokomo's own **Big Ben.** Ben was a crossbred Hereford steer who at the time of his birth in 1902 was proclaimed to be the largest calf in the world. When you see Ben, you won't find it hard to believe. At four years of age the steer weighed 4,720 pounds, stood 6 feet 4 inches tall, measured 13 feet 6 inches in girth, and was an astonishing 16 feet 8 inches from his nose to the tip of his tail. For many years he was exhibited around the country in circuses and sideshows. He had to be destroyed in 1911 after breaking his leg, and shortly thereafter he was stuffed. Today he shares a place of honor with another of Kokomo's giant wonders—**the stump of a huge sycamore tree.** The stump—12 feet tall and 51 feet in circumference—is impressive enough, but it only hints at the magnificent tree of which it once was a part. Originally more than 100 feet in height, the tree grew to maturity on a farm west of Kokomo. Its hollow trunk once housed a telephone booth large enough to accommodate more than a dozen people at a time. When the tree was storm-damaged, around 1915, the enormous stump was pulled to the park by a house mover. Big Ben and the stump now occupy a building built specifically to display and protect them; (317) 452–0063.

The ◈ **Kokomo Opalescent Glass Company,** in operation since 1888, once supplied glass to Louis C. Tiffany. Today this small factory is known worldwide as a leading producer of fine art glass, and visitors can watch the glass-making process from beginning to end. Free tours at 10:00 A.M. Wednesday and Friday, except in December. An adjoining retail shop is open 9:00 A.M. to 5:00 P.M. Monday through Friday; Saturday hours vary. Located at 1310 South Market Street; (317) 457–8136.

HUNTINGTON COUNTY

One of Indiana's most famous sons, J. Danforth Quayle (better known as Dan), is the fifth Hoosier to serve as our country's vice president. Quayle was born in Indianapolis in 1947, but his family moved to Huntington about a year later, and it is Huntington that Quayle calls home.

When George Bush and Quayle launched their campaign for the White House in 1988, they came to the Huntington County Courthouse to do it. When Quayle and his wife, Marilyn, received their law degrees from Indiana University in Bloomington, they came to Huntington to open a law office. When Quayle first ran for public office in 1976 (as a U.S. Representative), he ran as a resident of Huntington.

In June 1993, Huntington demonstrated its affection for Quayle by opening the ◆ **Dan Quayle Center and Museum** at 815 Warren Street. Visitors will see exhibits from every phase of Quayle's life, beginning with a newspaper clipping announcing his birth, a baby footprint taken at the hospital in which he was born, and a photo of newborn Quayle in a diaper. Of particular interest is Quayle's second-grade report card, boasting all As and Bs. A copy of Quayle's college diploma is missing a few pieces, thanks to a family dog (a photo of the offender, much loved regardless, is framed with the diploma). And no museum honoring Dan Quayle would be complete without some golf memorabilia; an old golf bag and photos of a teenage Quayle holding trophies won in a junior tournament are among them.

You'll know when you get to Huntington. It would be hard to miss the sign at the city limits that proclaims this to be HUNTINGTON: HOME OF THE 44TH VICE PRESIDENT DAN QUAYLE.

The museum is open 10:00 A.M. to 4:00 P.M. Tuesday through Saturday and 1:00 to 4:00 P.M. Sunday. Free admission, but donations are welcome. Contact the museum at P.O. Box 856, Huntington 46750; (219) 356–6356.

After you've toured Dan Quayle's museum, stop by and see **Hy Goldenberg's Outhouses.** You won't see any signs honoring Hy's outhouses, but the town is fond of them just the same.

Hy purchased his first two outhouses some thirty years ago for strictly utilitarian reasons. He and his wife were building a home in a then-isolated spot on the banks of the Wabash River, and they needed a toilet the carpenters could use while working on the house. Since then, Hy has come to regard outhouses as an important segment of Americana, and his collection now numbers twelve.

Although most of the outhouses are variations of the typical square wooden ones, Hy also has an octagon-shaped concrete one. A three-seater model boasts a child-size seat in the middle for the family that enjoys togetherness.

Hy points out the fact that building outhouses was a source of employment for many men during the Great Depression. Although comfort and safety were certainly important considerations, beauty was not ignored either. Many were covered with roses and trellises to please the lady of the house.

Visitors are welcome to tour the unusual collection free of charge, but because the outhouses are on private property, please phone Nan Rosenberg before visiting. You will be given exact directions when you call; (219) 356–4467.

KOSCIUSKO COUNTY

Some towns will do almost anything to get attention. Mentone grabbed its share of publicity by erecting a monument unique in the world. There it stands, right next to Main Street—a 12-foot-high, 3,000-pound **concrete egg.** If, when in Mentone, anyone should ask the perennial puzzler "Which came first, the chicken or the egg?" the answer would almost certainly have to be "the egg." Pity the poor chicken who would have to handle this one!

In 1946, when the monument was first "laid," every farmer in the area had a chicken house, and eggs were shipped all over the Midwest. That enterprise declined in the 1950s, but the lives of the town's 950 residents continue to be intertwined with eggs and chickens. Local businesses hatch eggs, provide chicken meat for soup companies, and separate egg whites from the yolks for bakeries. And each June the community celebrates industry, heritage, and monument with an egg festival. Contact the Mentone Chamber of Commerce, P.O. Box 365, Mentone 46539; (219) 353–7551.

Next to the city park on Oak Street, just south of State Road 25 West in Mentone, you'll find the ◆ **Lawrence D. Bell Aircraft Museum.** It contains the memorabilia of Larry Bell, the Mentone native who forsook eggs and instead founded the Bell Aircraft Corporation. Bell produced twenty aviation firsts, including the world's first commercial helicopter and the nation's first jet-propelled airplane. Scale models of many Bell aircraft are on display. Guided tours are offered from 1:00 to 5:00 P.M. Sunday from Memorial Day weekend through Labor Day; other times by appointment. Nominal admission fee; contact the museum at P.O. Box 411, Mentone 46539; (219) 353–7551.

In honor of Kosciusko County's agricultural heritage, the Greater Warsaw Area Chamber of Commerce has put together two drive-yourself farm tours. Scenic country roads lead visitors past farms that produce chickens, buffalo, llamas, pigs, sheep, and cattle, as well as spearmint and various fruits and vegetables. Maple Leaf Farms is the largest producer of ducklings in the country and maybe the world. Ault Stables trains harness horses. Many facilities offer guided tours by prearrangement. Free maps are available at the Kosciusko County Convention and Visitors Bureau, 313 South Buffalo Street, Warsaw 46580; (800) 800–6090 or (219) 269–6090.

The largest of only five such gardens in the United States, the ◈ **Warsaw Biblical Gardens** cover three-quarters of an acre in Warsaw's Center Lake Park. All plants mentioned in the Bible have been meticulously researched for this project, and thus far about sixty of the eighty-five identified varieties have been acquired.

An oasis of tranquility, the gardens are enclosed by a low field-stone wall. Visitors can meander along stone paths that lead through six distinct plant environs: meadow, crop, orchard, forest, brook, and desert. A plaque for each of the species identifies the plant and its biblical reference.

Water lilies, yellow iris, and sweet flag adorn a water garden that's shaded by an umbrella palm. A unique wooden arbor was designed by famous craftsman David Robinson, who served as the first coordinator for the restoration of New York City's Central Park before going into business for himself. Grapevines planted when the gardens were dedicated in June 1991 now nearly obscure the arbor, creating a cool, shaded retreat on hot summer days.

The gardens, located at the intersection of State Road 15 North and Canal Street, are open free of charge from dawn to dusk, April through October. For additional information contact the Warsaw Community Development Corporation, P.O. Box 1223, Warsaw 46580; (219) 267–6419.

LAGRANGE COUNTY

No place in this country has done better by its junk than the tiny hamlet of Shipshewana. Each Tuesday and Wednesday from May through October, it puts on what may be the biggest small-town sale in the country. Anything you've ever wanted has almost certainly, at one time or another, been available at the ◈ **Shipshewana** (Shipshe for short) **Auction and Flea Market.** The items available at one recent sale included old beer cans, garden tools, round oak tables, new hats and clothing at discount prices, door-knobs, bubble-gum machines, rare books, antique china, long-legged underwear, fenceposts, Aladdin lamps, fishing rods, parts for old wagons, extra pieces for a Lionel train set, hand and power tools, quilts, a worn-out butter churn, a half-full can of green house paint, baseball cards, homemade toy alligators, and—perhaps the most unusual item ever offered here—a used tombstone.

Wednesday is the biggest business day. In addition to the flea market, held over from Tuesday, a livestock sale and a miscellaneous auction take place. The vast array of sale items keeps about a dozen auctioneers busy from 7:00 A.M. on throughout the afternoon, while in the livestock barn farmers do some hot-and-heavy bidding on 2,500 head of cattle, sheep, and pigs. Outside in the flea market yard, nearly 1,000 vendors display their wares. On an average Wednesday, $200,000 worth of livestock and goods changes hands, not including the several thousand dollars spent at the flea market. Although it would be a compliment to describe some of the merchandise as junk, there are also many valuable antiques and hard-to-find items.

The Shipshe Auction hosts as many as 30,000 visitors a day. License plates reveal they come from every state in the Union and Canada. When winter comes the flea market closes down, but the Wednesday auction simply moves under cover and continues throughout the year.

Each Friday the auction yard is the scene of a horse auction that draws buyers and sellers from all over North America to deal in Amish draft horses, reputed to be some of the finest in the land. (Shipshewana sits right in the heart of one of the largest Amish settlements in the United States.)

You'll have a grand time at the Shipshe Auction even if you don't buy a thing. It's one of the world's great spectator events. The auction yards are located on State Road 5 at the south edge of Shipshewana. For more details contact the Shipshewana Auction and Flea Market, Box 185, Shipshewana 46565; (219) 768-4129.

Since all the people who attend Shipshe's various auctions have to eat, a special **Auction Restaurant,** operated from one of the sale barns, is open three days a week in the summer. It dishes up delicious Amish food nonstop from 5:00 A.M. to 7:00 P.M. Tuesday and Wednesday and from 5:00 A.M. until the horse sales close for the day on Friday (open Wednesday and Friday only during winter months); (219) 768-4129.

Another fine Amish meal can be had at the **Buggy Wheel**

Restaurant on Morton Street in downtown Shipshewana. Some of the more unusual breakfast fare includes mush, headcheese, and, on Thursday only, tomato gravy, but there are plenty of eggs, bacon, and potatoes on hand, too. All lunches are served cafeteria style, while a soup, salad, and dessert buffet is a specialty on Friday and Saturday evenings. Not all meals are offered every day. Open 5:00 A.M. to 7:00 P.M. Monday through Thursday and 5:00 A.M. to 8:00 P.M. Friday and Saturday, May through October; winter hours vary; (219) 768–4444.

To learn more about the Mennonite/Amish lifestyle and heritage, explore the fascinating exhibits at the ◆ **Menno-Hof Visitors Center** on State Road 5 South opposite the Shipshewana Auction grounds. Of particular interest is a booth where visitors actually "feel, see, and hear" a simulated tornado. Admission by donation. Generally open 10:00 A.M. to 5:00 P.M. Monday through Saturday; hours may be seasonally adjusted. Call (219) 768–4117.

Stretching along Pigeon River in northeastern Lagrange County and reaching eastward into Steuben County is the 11,500-acre **Pigeon River State Fish and Wildlife Area.** The hauntingly beautiful stream, edged by lush vegetation choked with hyacinths, flows through an outstanding variety of habitats—marshes, meadows, woods, swamps, and bogs. Birdwatchers love this area; some 216 species of birds, many of them rare, have been sighted here. In the spring and early summer, wildflowers run rampant. It's all reminiscent of the Southland's fabled Suwannee River—a fine and private place in which to study nature; canoe; hunt mushrooms, nuts, and berries; hike; fish; pitch a tent; or cross-country ski.

The **Tamarack Bog State Nature Preserve** near the center of the wildlife area contains the largest tamarack swamp in Indiana and harbors such unique plants as the insectivorous pitcher plant and sundew. Contact the Pigeon River State Fish and Wildlife Area, Box 71, Mongo 46771; (219) 367–2164.

MIAMI COUNTY

The circus first came to Peru, Indiana, in the late 1800s, and it remains there to this day, the single most dominant force in the community.

It all began with native son Ben Wallace, who owned a livery stable in Peru. One winter a broken-down animal show limped into town and found shelter in Ben's stable. When spring came, Ben was left with all the animals in lieu of a fee. Using his Hoosier ingenuity, Ben spiffed things up a bit, started his own circus, and built it into one of the world's finest—the Hagenbeck-Wallace Circus. Winter quarters were set up on the vast farm fields just outside of town, and other major circuses of the day, lured by the excellent facilities, also came to Peru in the off-season.

Among the show business greats who spent at least part of the year here were Clyde Beatty, the noted animal trainer (like Ben Wallace, a native son); Emmett Kelly, the renowned clown; Willi Wilno, "the human cannonball"; and Tom Mix, who later starred in Hollywood westerns. Red Skelton left his home in southern Indiana when he was just a boy to join the Hagenbeck-Wallace Circus and to launch one of the most famous and enduring careers in the entertainment business.

The circus—and Peru with it—flourished for many years before passing into near oblivion, but local folks, many of them direct descendants of stars who brightened the firmament of circus history, decided that their town's unique heritage should be preserved forever. And so each year in the third week of July, the circus once again comes to Peru.

The performers, who must be residents of Miami County, range in age from six to their twenties, and they are so skillful you'll find it difficult to believe that this is not a professional show. Since the children of Peru are to the circus born—beginning their training in earliest childhood under the tutelage of some of the finest circus pros in the country—a constant supply of new talent is available. All the components of the old-time circus are here—aerialists, clowns, tightrope walkers, human pyramids, gymnasts, animal trainers, and much more. The whole thing is so authentic and entertaining that NBC Television once filmed an hour-long documentary about it.

There are several performances during the annual festival, as well as a giant parade complete with calliopes, old circus wagons, and the rousing music of the Circus City Band. For additional information contact the Circus City Festival Office, 154 North Broadway, Peru 46970; (317) 472–3918.

One of the finest collections of circus relics in the world is housed in Peru's new ✦ **International Circus Hall of Fame.**

Admission fee. At this writing, hours vary. Call (317) 472–7553 for up-to-date information.

Even in death Ben Wallace chose to remain in Peru. He is buried in **Mount Hope Cemetery** on Twelfth Street, along with another well-known native son, Cole Porter. One of the few song-writers who wrote both words and music, Porter penned such classics as "Night and Day," "When They Begin the Beguine," "I've Got You Under My Skin," and "What Is This Thing Called Love?" The Miami County Historical Society—(317) 472–3901, extension 40—can direct you to Porter's birthplace, his mother's home, and his grandmother's home. None are open to the public, but they can be seen from the road.

Although Cole Porter is gone, the chocolate fudge he loved lingers on. A trip to Peru always included a visit to **Arnold's Candy Store** at 288 East Main Street, where Mr. Porter purchased a goodly supply of his favorite confection to take with him wherever he went. The store has changed ownership since then, but the fudge is still made from the original recipe. Open 9:00 A.M. to 5:00 P.M. Monday through Saturday; (317) 473–5363.

RANDOLPH COUNTY

At the **Silver Towne Coin Shop** in Winchester, all that glitters *is* gold—or silver—and the beautiful antique-decorated show-rooms in which the collections are displayed are as dazzling as the shop's wares. Open 9:00 A.M. to 5:00 P.M. Monday through Friday and 9:00 A.M. to 4:00 P.M. Saturday. Located just west of U.S. Highway 27 on the north side of Union Street; (317) 584–7481.

People from all over the world flock to Winchester each July to attend the **International Hawaiian Steel Guitar Convention.** For three days the air is filled with music, and on Saturday night everyone's invited to a luau. Contact Charles Moore, RR 1, Winchester 47394, (317) 584–6746, or the Winchester Area Chamber of Commerce, 213½ South Main Street, Winchester 47394; (317) 584–3731.

STEUBEN COUNTY

Majestic **Potawatomi Inn,** the only state park inn in northern Indiana, is one of the finest in the system. Resembling an Old

English lodge, it sits in a clearing on the shore of Lake James in 1,200-acre ◆ **Pokagon State Park** in Angola.

Winter is king here, and the main treat is a refrigerated, ¼-mile-long toboggan slide, generally open from Thanksgiving Day through February, that whisks you over the hills and through the woods at 35–40 miles per hour. In this snowy park tucked into the northeastern corner of the Hoosier State, winter visitors will also find an ice-skating pond, a sledding hill, and cross-country ski trails. Toboggans and cross-country ski equipment can be rented in the park.

After frolicking in the chilly outdoors all day, retire to the inn for a sauna and whirlpool bath, do a few laps in the indoor pool, or bask in the warmth of the redbrick fireplace.

The inn features more than eighty rooms, including some nearby sleeping cabins, and serves three meals daily in its highly-rated dining room. The atmosphere is so down-homey that guests often come to eat in their stocking feet. Roast beef is a daily feature on a dinner menu that usually includes a choice of seafood, steak, and a chicken or ham dish. The rates are hard to beat—from $39.00 to $57.00 a night for a double room and from $3.00 to $9.00 for dinner, with lunch and breakfast rates even cheaper.

Although Pokagon State Park and its inn have gained a reputation as a winter resort, people also come here in other seasons, when the forests and the sweeping lawns of the inn are a lush green, park lakes are ice-free for swimmers and fishermen, and park trails accommodate hikers instead of skiers. Horses can be rented at the saddle barn, and the tennis and basketball courts see heavy use.

The Nature Center is popular year-round, with naturalists always on hand to interpret each of nature's moods. Bison and elk reside in nearby pens. One park trail leads to the marshes, swamps, and forests of the **Potawatomi State Nature Preserve.** The largest known tamarack and yellow birch trees in the state, the only northern white cedars known to exist in Indiana, and several species of wild orchids grow within the preserve's 208 acres.

For information about either the park or the inn, write Pokagon State Park, 450 Lane 100, Lake James, Angola 46703; the park's phone is (219) 833–2012, the inn's is (219) 833–1077. To reach the park go west from Angola on U.S. Highway 20 to I–69.

Turn north on I–69 and proceed to State Road 727; State Road 727 leads west from I–69 to the park entrance.

All of Steuben County is noted for its natural beauty. Its combination of 101 lakes and verdant forests have earned it the nickname "Switzerland of Indiana," and no less an impresario than P. T. Barnum once pronounced Lake James "the most beautiful body of water I have ever seen!" What's more, Steuben County contains more dedicated state nature preserves than any other county in the state; you can learn more about them by contacting the Department of Natural Resources, Division of Nature Preserves, 402 West Washington Street, Room W267, Indianapolis 46204; (317) 232–4052.

NORTHWEST INDIANA

1. France Park
2. Portland Arch State Nature Preserve
3. Fulton County Museum
4. Jasper-Pulaski State Fish & Wildlife Area
5. German Methodist Cemetery Prairie
6. Hoosier Prairie State Nature Preserve
7. Carmelite Shrines
8. Old Lake County Court House
9. *SS Constantine* and Helen Greek Orthodox Cathedral
10. Hesston Steam Museum
11. LaPorte County Museum
12. Barker Civic Center
13. Old Lighthouse Museum
14. Washington Park Zoo
15. Antique Motorcycle Museum
16. Black Horse Troop
17. Shades State Park
18. Old Jail Museum
19. Ben Hur Museum
20. Indiana Dunes National Lakeshore
21. Indiana Dunes State Park
22. Wizard of Oz Museum
23. Chapel of the Resurrection
24. University of Notre Dame
25. Studebaker National Museum
26. East Race Waterway
27. Shiojiri Niwa
28. Tippecanoe Battlefield State Memorial
29. Wolf Park

Northwest Indiana

Cass County

The pride of Logansport is its turn-of-the-century **carousel.** Now nearly 100 years old, it is one of only two all-wood, hand-carved merry-go-rounds still operating in Indiana. (The other is in the Indianapolis Children's Museum.) Delighted riders compete for a mount on the outer side and the chance to snag the coveted brass ring as the carousel spins round and round. Their brightly colored steeds— a mix of thirty-one horses, three goats, three reindeer, three giraffes, a lion, and a tiger—were produced in 1892 by the talented hands of German craftsman Gustav A. Dentzel, who moved to the United States in 1860 and became this country's chief carousel maker.

Although the carousel is owned by a nonprofit citizens' group, a small fee is charged for each ride to help offset maintenance costs. You'll find the merry-go-round in **Riverside City Park,** located along the south bank of Eel River at 1300 Riverside Drive—just follow the sound of music. It operates daily 6:30 to 9:30 P.M. Monday through Saturday and 12:30 to 9:30 P.M. Sunday, Memorial Day through Labor Day. Contact the Logansport/Cass County Chamber of Commerce, 300 East Broadway, Logansport 46947; (219) 753–6388.

Four miles west of Logansport off U.S. Highway 24 you'll come upon ◆ **France Park** and its picturesque swimming hole. An abandoned stone quarry, partly hemmed in by precipitous cliffs, is filled with clear, brisk water that's irresistible on a hot summer day. Scuba and cliff divers like it, too.

Patches of woodland and a mossy, 15-foot waterfall on Paw Paw Creek add touches of beauty to the 500-acre county park. Visitors will also find a water slide, miniature golf course, more than 800 campsites, and, near the entrance, a century-old log cabin. Nominal admission fee; beach open Memorial Day through Labor Day; park open daily year-round 9:00 A.M. to 11:00 P.M. Contact France Park, RR 6, Logansport 46947; (219) 753–2928.

Fountain County

It will never give the folks in Utah anything to worry about, but Indiana does have a stone arch that's so unique it's been declared both a National Natural Landmark and a state nature preserve. Through the years the meanderings of a tiny stream in northwestern Fountain County have carved a 30-by-12-foot opening through a massive sandstone formation and created a natural bridge known as ◆ **Portland Arch.** Nearby Bear Creek flows through a deep ravine edged by rugged sandstone cliffs. The rare bush honeysuckle grows here, and this is the only known site in the state where the Canada blueberry is found. At times a cover of mosses and lichens and several species of ferns growing in the crevices of the cliffs create a landscape of green velvet. A quaint pioneer cemetery on the 253-acre preserve contains eleven marked graves.

Portland Arch State Nature Preserve is located on the south side of the town of Fountain. Signs lead the way to the preserve and two parking lots, each adjoined by a self-guiding trail. The loop trail leading from the first and main parking lot follows a hilly route about 1 mile long to Portland Arch. For additional information contact the Department of Natural Resources, Division of Nature Preserves, 402 West Washington Street, Room W267, Indianapolis 46204; (317) 232–4052.

Fulton County

Fulton County is peppered with round barns, the legacy of a turn-of-the-century fad. At last count nine of the original barns, the newest of which was built in 1924, were still standing. They are kept in excellent repair and are both unusual and beautiful to behold. No two are alike. The main idea behind this flurry of round-barn building was to create one centralized feeding station for livestock, thus increasing the efficiency of the farmer's operation. The barns proved to be impractical to heat and light in those days, however, and the idea was abandoned.

In 1988 the ◆ **Fulton County Museum** near Rochester opened its doors to the public. A round barn, rebuilt on the premises, opened in 1990. Together they offer a glimpse into the county's past and provide information about its unique heritage. Maps are available for a drive-yourself tour of the county's barns. Although officially the barns are not open to the public, many owners, if they're at home when you arrive, are happy to show you through their barns, and several barns are open to the public

Round Barn at Fulton County Museum

during the third weekend in June when the county celebrates a Round Barn Festival. Admission to the museum is free; open 9:00 A.M. to 5:00 P.M. Monday through Saturday. Contact the museum at 37 East 375 North, Rochester 46975; (219) 223–4436.

JASPER COUNTY

Each fall one of Indiana's most magnificent natural spectacles takes place at the 8,000-acre ❖ **Jasper-Pulaski State Fish and Wildlife Area.** During the last week in October and the first week in November, some 12,000 greater sandhill cranes pause here to rest on their annual journey south for the winter. Jasper-Pulaski is believed to be the only place east of the Mississippi River where this unusual species stops en masse during migration.

These beautiful blue-gray birds, which stand about 3½ feet tall and have a wingspan of up to 7 feet, are as impressive to hear as they are to look at. The best times to view them are at dawn, when they rise up from the misty marshes and call to one another in noisy unison, and again at sunset, when they return to the marsh for the night.

You can pick up literature about the cranes and obtain a free observation permit at the area headquarters, then continue on to one of two observation towers.

The cranes also migrate through Jasper-Pulaski between late February and mid-April, but they are usually present in greater concentration in the fall.

Although the sandhills are the main attraction, other wildlife species are here as well. Canada geese, quail, woodcock, and deer live in the wild year-round, and elk and bison roam fenced-in pastures. Part of Jasper-Pulaski serves as a game farm where pheasant are reared as stock for fish and wildlife areas throughout the state. Natural history and wildlife exhibits are maintained in one of the service buildings, and hiking trails wind through the area.

Located in the area's northwest corner is the 480-acre **Tefft Savanna State Nature Preserve,** home to many plants that are extremely rare in the Midwest. The entire fish and wildlife area actually occupies parts of three counties—Jasper, Pulaski, and Starke—but the majority of its 8,000 acres are in Jasper County. It's open daily year-round at all times, and entrance is free. The headquarters office is open 7:00 A.M. to 3:30 P.M. Monday through Friday, but hours may be extended in certain seasons.

To reach the refuge go north from Medaryville (in Pulaski County) on U.S. Highway 421 and turn west onto State Road 143; proceed 1½ miles to the entrance on the right side of the road; follow the signs. Contact Jasper-Pulaski State Fish and Wildlife Area, RR 1, Box 216, Medaryville 47957; (219) 843–4841.

LAKE COUNTY

When the first white settlers came to Indiana, seven-eighths of the land was covered with a forest so dense that a squirrel could visit every tree in the state without ever once touching the ground. The far northwest corner, including what is now Lake County, was a sea of grass—grass so tall in places that a rider on horseback could not be seen above it. It was a long time before man realized the value of saving some remnants of that original landscape, and by then most of it was irretrievably gone.

Two of the finest examples still in existence can be seen in Lake County. ◆ **German Methodist Cemetery Prairie** covers just one acre at the rear of the cemetery for which it's named, but more than eighty rare and vanishing plant species thrive in its rich black soil. In late summer, when most of them are in bloom, it is a place of incredible beauty.

This tiny preserve is probably the most botanically diverse acre in Indiana. You'll find it in the midst of farm fields on the east side of U.S. Highway 41, 1 mile south of the intersection of U.S. Highway 41 and 141st Street in Cedar Lake. The old cemetery is still there and should be respected. Behind it is the prairie, surrounded by a chain-link fence to protect the fragile plant life. For additional information contact The Nature Conservancy, Indiana Field Office, 1330 West Thirty-eighth Street, Indianapolis 46208; (317) 923–7547.

◆ **Hoosier Prairie,** the largest virgin prairie in Indiana, sprawls over 439 acres near Griffith. It contains some 300 species of native plants, including grasses that reach 12 feet in height. A trail about 2 miles long leads through some of the preserve's less sensitive areas and permits a look at the diverse habitats. You may even spot a deer along the way. Hoosier Prairie, a state nature preserve, is located west of Griffith on the south side of Main Street; a small parking lot is near the trailhead. Open daily year-round during daylight hours; free. Contact the Department of National Resources, Division of Nature Preserves, 402 West Washington Street, Room W267, Indianapolis 46204; (317) 232–4052.

The ◆ **Carmelite Shrines** in Munster offer a haven of serenity. On the grounds are twenty shrines that display Italian sculptures in a grotto studded with crystals and unusual rocks. The overall effect is enhanced by special lighting. You'll also find an arboretum and, in the monastery, a replica of the Vatican's Private Audience Hall. Grounds are open free of charge 1:00 to 5:00 P.M. daily, weather permitting; building interiors can usually be seen on request. The shrines are located at 1628 Ridge Road, ½ mile west of U.S. Highway 41; (219) 838–9657.

When hunger pangs strike, head for **Teibel's Restaurant** in Schererville. Teibel's first opened its doors in 1929, the year the stock market crashed and launched the Great Depression. That the restaurant operated continuously through all those lean years and still thrives today should tell you something. One reason for its longevity is that the old family recipe for fried chicken, which initially earned the restaurant its reputation, is a winner. The chicken (as well as fried perch) is served on an all-you-can-eat basis. Prices are moderate. Open 11:00 A.M. to 10:00 P.M. Sunday through Thursday and 11:00 A.M. to 2:00 A.M. Friday and Saturday. Located at the corner of U.S. Highways 41 and 30; (219) 865–2000.

Crown Point is dominated by the "Grand Old Lady of Lake County," the magnificent ◆ **Old Lake County Court House** that many regard as Indiana's most impressive. Built in 1878, it served as the seat of county government until 1974. Today it houses more than twenty crafts and specialty shops, including a fascinating puzzle shop and the Women's Exchange Resale Shop (profits aid courthouse restoration), as well as the Lake County Historical Museum. Don't miss its arched brick ceilings and intriguing hallways. The courthouse is located at the corner of Joliet and Court streets; its shops are generally open from 10:00 A.M. to 5:00 P.M. Monday through Friday. The museum is open noon to 4:00 P.M. Friday through Sunday, spring through fall; other times by appointment. Nominal admission fee for museum; (219) 663–0660.

In 1896 William Jennings Bryan stood on the courthouse steps and campaigned for the presidency. A then-unknown car designer, Louis Chevrolet, came here to accept the winner's cup for the first major auto race in the United States, a race held in 1909 that was the forerunner of the Indy 500. From 1916 to 1941 the courthouse became famous for its instant marriages; the usual blood test and three-day waiting period were not required here. Among the thousands married at the courthouse during that period were Joe DiMaggio, Red Grange, Colleen Moore, Tom Mix, Ronald Reagan, and, at the height of his career, Rudolph Valentino.

The magnificent ◆ **SS Constantine and Helen Greek Orthodox Cathedral** rises from amid thirty-seven acres of grounds at 8000 Madison Street in Merrillville. The only such church in the state, it features twenty-five large stained-glass windows, Byzantine mosaic work, and a rotunda 100 feet in diameter and 50 feet in height. Open 9:00 A.M. to 5:00 P.M. Monday through Friday and 10:00 A.M. to 2:00 P.M. Saturday. Each year on the second weekend of July, a Grecian festival takes place here; (219) 769–2481.

Until recently, the city of Gary was known as Steeltown, U.S.A., but it is perhaps better known now as the **birthplace of Michael Jackson,** the phenomenon of the 1980s. Throughout the city, billboards proclaim that Michael Jackson is "Another Great Gary Product," as well as the "World's Number One Enter-tainer." Michael was born here in August 1958 and grew up in a small, two-bedroom house located at 2300 Jackson Street (named long ago in honor of President Andrew Jackson). Although it's not open to the public, the house can be viewed from the street. Many folks hereabouts still remember the Jackson Five's first pub-lic appearance on the stage of Gary's Roosevelt High School in 1965. Shy Michael had to be dragged onto the stage, but what happened from that moment on is show business history.

The frogs legs served at **Phil Smidt & Son** in Hammond have been celebrated for all of the more than seventy-five years the restaurant has been in business. Once the frogs legs were gathered from the shore of nearby Lake Michigan; today they, like all frogs legs served in restaurants in the United States, come from Bangladesh. They are still delicious, however, and what's more, they're served in a stunning room. One side is open, two walls are a soft rose hue, and the third bears murals of gigantic roses done in high-gloss paint on a shiny black background. Soft light filters through blocks of aquarium glass. The white tablecloths are bor-dered in pink, and each place is set with rose-colored napkins and rose-embossed water glasses. Be sure to ask to be seated in the Rose Room; there are five other dining rooms as well.

Another specialty of the house is lake perch, served whole or boned and cooked to perfection. Top off your meal with warm gooseberry pie.

Outside, freight trains rumble by, and smokestacks spew smoke—an incredible contrast to the beauty within.

You'll find Phil Smidt & Son at 1205 North Calumet Avenue; it's open for lunch and dinner from 11:15 A.M. to 9:00 P.M. Mon-day through Thursday and 11:15 A.M. to 10:00 P.M. Friday and Saturday; (219) 659–0025.

LaPorte County

At the tiny town of Hesston, on County Road 1000N, northeast of LaPorte, you can see the ◆ **Hesston Steam Museum.** Spread out over a 155-acre site is an assemblage of steam-powered equipment worth several million dollars—trains, cranes, buzz saws, and a boat among them. You can take a 2-mile ride on a steam train or watch a miniature train, authentic to the tiniest detail, whiz by on a 3½-inch track. Feel free to toot a horn or ring a bell—it's that type of place.

You can walk through the exhibit any day except Monday, but the equipment is in operation noon to 5:00 P.M. on Saturday, Sunday, and holidays, Memorial Day weekend through Labor Day, and Sunday only from Labor Day through October. An especially exuberant celebration takes place during the Annual Labor Day Weekend Steam Show. The outdoor museum is located at 1201 East County Road 1000N, approximately 2½ miles east of State Road 39. Admission is free except during special events; a nominal fee is charged at all times for train rides. Contact the LaPorte County Historical Steam Society at 2940 Mt. Claire Way, Long Beach, Michigan City 46360; (219) 872–7405 or (800) 634–2650.

In the town of LaPorte you can take a free tour of the ✦ **LaPorte County Museum.** The more than 20,000 items on exhibit include the W. A. Jones collection of antique firearms and weapons—recognized as the best collection of its kind in the United States and one of the three best in the world. There's also a folklore display that tells the story of Belle Gunness, LaPorte's Madam Bluebeard, who in the early 1900s lured at least a dozen men to her farm north of town by promising to marry them; once there, the would-be husbands were promptly killed for their money and buried in the farmyard. The museum, located adjacent to the county courthouse, is open free of charge 10:00 A.M. to 4:30 P.M. Monday through Friday and 1:00 to 4:00 P.M. the first Sunday of each month (closed holidays); (219) 326–6808, extension 276.

At the **Angelo Bernacchi Greenhouses,** you can treat your visual and olfactory senses to the thousands of growing green things that make this the largest grower and retailer of plants in the entire Midwest. There are acres to browse through all year long. The retail shop is open 9:00 A.M. to 5:00 P.M. Monday through Saturday; special tours on May 1 and December 1. Located at 1010 Fox Street, LaPorte; (219) 362–6202.

The ✦ **Barker Civic Center** at 631 Washington Street in Michigan City exudes turn-of-the-century elegance. Once the home of millionaire industrialist John H. Barker, it contains thirty-eight rooms; ten bathrooms; several fireplaces with hand-carved teak, walnut, or mahogany woodwork; and a mirrored ballroom. Adjacent to the library terrace is a sunken Italian garden. Tours at 10:00 A.M., 11:30 A.M., and 1:00 P.M. Monday through Friday year-round; also at noon and 2:00 P.M. Saturday and Sunday, June through October; closed major holidays. Nominal admission fee; (219) 873–1520.

Not far away a fishing pier that extends into Lake Michigan offers a view of Indiana's only operating lighthouse. On a clear day you can also see the Chicago skyline.

The area's natural history is explored at the ◆ **Old Light-house Museum** in **Washington Park,** Michigan City's ninety-acre lakefront park. Situated on Heisman Harbor Road at the

Old Lighthouse Museum

park's west entrance, the museum contains a rare Fourth Order Fresnel lens, shipbuilding tools, and other maritime artifacts. Open 1:00 to 4:00 P.M. Tuesday through Sunday, year-round; closed Monday and holidays. Nominal admission charge; (219) 872–6133 or 872–3273.

◆ **The Washington Park Zoo** features more than 180 species of animals and raises more Bengal tigers than any other zoo in the United States. Within its boundaries an observation tower atop a dune offers spectacular bird's-eye views. The zoo is open daily 10:30 A.M. to 6:00 P.M., March through December; 10:30 A.M. to 3:00 P.M. daily the rest of the year; nominal admission fee; (219) 873–1510.

MARSHALL COUNTY

Larry Feece started collecting motorcycles in 1960, when he was just a teenager. Today he owns more than 300 bikes, a sizable collection that over the years outgrew both his house and his wife's patience. So Larry developed the ◆ **Antique Motorcycle Museum,** believed to be the only museum in the country devoted entirely to motorcycles. At any given time about half of the still-growing collection, which includes an 1899 Peugeot (Larry's oldest bike), an original Johnson Motorbike, and a 1934 motorcycle James brought over from England, is on display. Open 9:00 A.M. to 5:00 P.M. Saturday and Sunday, April through October; nominal admission fee. Located at 139 East Walnut Street in Argos; (219) 892–5177 (museum) or 935–2477 (twenty-four-hour answering service).

Since the U.S. Army Cavalry was disbanded in 1950, the ◆ **Black Horse Troop** of Culver Military Academy (a college preparatory boarding school in the town of Culver) has been the nation's largest mounted military organization. The 144 young men who compose its ranks hone their skills in the academy's extensive horsemanship programs. Organized in 1897, the troop has taken part in eight presidential inaugurations, escorted kings and queens, and been featured in major horse shows throughout the country, but you can see it free, with all its pomp and pageantry, each Sunday afternoon from May through October. That's when the troopers don their military dress, mount their black steeds, and parade across the Academy's well-kept grounds.

While you're there, pick up a map at the administration office and tour the 1,500-acre campus, beautifully situated near the shoreline of Lake Maxinkuckee. Contact Culver Military Academy, CEF 129, Culver 46511; (219) 842–3311.

MONTGOMERY COUNTY

For sheer natural beauty it's hard to beat ◆ **Shades State Park** near Waveland, but to fully appreciate its magnificent scenery and outstanding geologic features you'll have to do some hiking. Only by taking to the trails can you see the primeval terrain for which the park is noted. Some first-time hikers do a double take when they see what awaits them—a landscape like this just isn't associated with Indiana.

About 470 acres of the 3,000-acre park have been set aside as the **Pine Hills State Nature Preserve.** Within its boundaries are four narrow rock ridges from 75 to 100 feet tall that are recognized as the finest example of incised meanders in the eastern United States. This observation was made by no less an authority than the National Park Service, which designated the preserve a National Natural Landmark.

Native white pine and hemlock, not usually found this far south, are relics of a long-ago past when this area was much cooler. The arrival of spring is first announced by the flowering of the rare snow trillium, and the coloring of the land continues through May, when the dogwoods and redbuds show off their blossoms. Through it all flows Sugar Creek, the most beautiful stream in the state.

When our forefathers first cast eyes on the lush forests and deep gorges along Sugar Creek, they referred to this place as "the Shades of Death." The long shadows cast by the heavy growth of trees initially appeared ominous to them, but as they became more familiar with the area the nickname was shortened to "the Shades." It remains appropriate to this day since the land has remained virtually untouched by human hands.

Two other impressive features are Silver Cascade Falls, one of eleven waterfalls in the park, and Devil's Punchbowl, a large, circular grotto cut into the sandstone by two small streams.

Canoeists take to Sugar Creek in droves, and if you're into solitude you'll want to avoid a trip on summer weekends. Weekdays in May or June or any day in August or September when the water level is down promises quieter floats. The most scenic stretch, which lies between Shades State Park and Turkey Run State Park (located to the southwest in adjoining Parke County), can be seen in one day. Put in at Deer's Mill Covered Bridge, which spans Sugar Creek along State Road 234 on the eastern edge of Shades State Park. For an enjoyable two-day trip, put in at Elston Park in Crawfordsville. Both trips end at West Union Covered Bridge in Parke County. Always check water conditions at park headquarters before starting out, however; the creek can be dangerous at flood stage.

Although most of the park is undeveloped, visitors will find more than one hundred primitive campsites, special campgrounds for backpackers and canoeists, and several picnic areas, some with shelters. Bicycles can be rented in the park, and a naturalist is on duty in the summer.

Shades State Park is located along both banks of Sugar Creek in southwestern Montgomery County and spills over into Parke County. The entrance is on County Road 800S, just west of State Road 234; look for signs. Open daily year-round; nominal vehicle admission fee. Contact the property manager, Shades State Park, Route 1, Box 72, Waveland 47989; (317) 435-2810.

Just north of Shades State Park, County Road 875W leads north off State Road 234 to the Hoosier State's own **Alamo,** which the town's fifty residents hope you'll remember. There, on the outside front of an old school gymnasium, a local artist has created a series of colorful murals that depict both Alamos—the one in Texas and the one in Indiana.

Another small town in the northwestern corner of the county has recently achieved fame without even trying. When Hollywood came to Hoosierland looking for an idyllic rural area in which to film the principal exterior shots for the movie *Hoosiers,* it chose **New Richmond.** (For readers who missed it, *Hoosiers* is loosely based on the true story of a small-town high school basketball team that defied all odds to win the Indiana state championship.) Now tourists, enthralled with what they saw on the screen, travel here to see the real thing—the storefronts, the main street with its single traffic light, the farm fields bathed in sunset gold. The sign that identifies the community as New Richmond is now embellished with the words WELCOME TO HICKORY (the town's movie name), and the Hickory Festival, held in late September, features a basketball game and *Hoosiers* film clips.

For information about Alamo and New Richmond, contact the Montgomery County Visitors & Convention Bureau, 412 East Main Street, Crawfordsville 47933; (317) 362–5200 or (800) 866–3973.

The Old Montgomery County Jail at 225 North Washington Street in Crawfordsville was the first of only six rotary jails ever built worldwide and is the only one still operational. Completed in 1882, it remained in daily use until 1973. The cell blocks are arranged in a circle in such a way that the sheriff, with the turn of a crank, could rotate the cells around him and check on his prisoners without ever taking a step. Now known as the ✦ **Old Jail Museum,** it's open free of charge from 1:00 to 4:30 P.M. Wednesday through Sunday, April, May, September, and October; 10:00 A.M. to 4:30 P.M. Wednesday through Saturday and 1:00 to 4:30 P.M. Tuesday and Sunday, June through August; (317) 362–5222.

The campus of **Wabash College,** at the corner of West Wabash and Grant avenues in Crawfordsville, is of interest because of the mid-1800s architecture of its buildings and its arboretum of native Indiana trees. Students apparently find the setting conducive to learning. Out of 1,500 colleges and universities in this country, Wabash ranks sixteenth in the percentage of graduates who go on to earn Ph.D.s. Perhaps it's the lack of distraction—Wabash is an all-male college. Call (317) 362–1400.

Also in Crawfordsville, on the corner of Wallace Avenue and East Pike Street, you'll find a four-acre park that contains the ✦ **Ben Hur Museum** housed in the study of General Lew Wallace. Famed as a lawyer, statesman, and Civil War general, Wallace is nevertheless probably best remembered as the author of the novel *Ben Hur.* His eclectic study, designed by Wallace himself, is a mix of French, Byzantine, Romanesque, and Greek styles. The 20-foot-tall bronze statue of Wallace that stands nearby is a replica of one that was unveiled in Washington, D.C., in 1910. Each year in mid-October, a Circus Maximus is staged on these grounds, complete with a chariot race and Greek food. Open 10:00 A.M. to 4:30 P.M. Wednesday through Saturday and 1:00 to 4:30 P.M. Tuesday and Sunday, April through October; nominal admission fee; (317) 362–5769.

PORTER COUNTY

Indiana does not have a Grand Canyon or a Yosemite, but it does have some of the largest sand dunes this side of the Sahara. Since 1972, most of them have been part of the 13,000-acre ◈ **Indiana Dunes National Lakeshore,** a miracle of survival in the midst of one of the most heavily industrialized regions in the country. Its lovely sand beaches along the southern shoreline of Lake Michigan are legendary for miles around, but they are only part of what can be seen and done here.

Mt. Baldy inches away from the lake each year; its name hints at why. Because it has not been stabilized by vegetation, the 135-foot-tall dune is kept in constant motion by wind and water, forcing the dune to take giant steps backward. Climb to the top for a sweeping view of Lake Michigan.

Not all of the landscape is sand and water. There are also grassy hills, patches of prairie, lush wetlands, and cool forests with a canopy so dense that sunlight barely filters through. Miller Woods, Cowles Bog, and Pinhook Bog would be exceptional natural areas anywhere, but their existence in the midst of such pollution, industry, and urban population is incredible.

The Bailly Homestead, dating to 1822, and the Chellberg Farm, built in the late 1880s, contain historical structures that the public can visit. There are hiking, bicycling, and horseback-riding trails to follow; in the winter they're used by cross-country skiers. At least 223 species of birds have been identified here, and many rare plants live among the dunes. Special programs and events are held all year long.

Although the national lakeshore actually lies in parts of three counties—Lake, Porter, and LaPorte—its visitor center is in Porter County, and this is where you should begin your visit. The center is located on Kemil Road, which runs south from U.S. Highway 12 about 3 miles east of the intersection of U.S. Highway 12 and State Road 49 near Porter, and is open daily year-round, 8:00 A.M. to 6:00 P.M. Memorial Day through Labor Day and 8:00 A.M. to 5:00 P.M. the rest of the year; closed major winter holidays. The park is open daily year-round; hours vary from area to area and are subject to change. A nominal parking fee is charged at West Beach from Memorial Day through Labor Day; everything else is free. For additional information contact Indiana Dunes National

Lakeshore, 1100 North Mineral Springs Road, Porter 46304; (219) 926–7561.

Completely surrounded by the national lakeshore are 2,182 acres that make up ◆ **Indiana Dunes State Park.** It offers a microcosm of the features found in its big brother and boasts the highest sand dune along the lakeshore—192-foot-tall Mt. Tom. The 1,500-acre **Dunes State Nature Preserve,** which lies within park boundaries, contains more species of trees than any other area of comparable size in the Midwest; from one spot alone you can identify thirty different varieties. In the summer the myriads of rare flowers and ferns found here create a near-tropical appearance. Recreational facilities include a modern campground, a nature center, a swimming beach, and trails for hiking, bicycling, and cross-country skiing. To reach the park proceed north from I–94 on State Road 49 for about 2 miles. The park is open year-round; a nominal vehicle admission fee is charged from spring through fall. Contact the Indiana Dunes State Park, 1600 North 25 East, Chesterton 46304; (218) 926–1952.

When the Chicago World's Fair of 1933 closed, five homes from the **"Houses of the Future" exhibit** were placed on a barge and transported across Lake Michigan to the then-new community of Beverly Shores. Plans to make Beverly Shores the ultimate vacation resort were thwarted by the lingering effects of the Great Depression, but the houses are still there, lined up along Lake Front Drive and still of interest. Especially startling is the House of Tomorrow, a twelve-sided structure built like a wedding cake (the top two floors are each smaller in circumference than the floor below). You'll also see a reproduction of Boston's Old North Church; it, too, was carted over from the fair. For more information contact the Porter County Convention, Recreation, and Visitors Commission, 800 Indian Boundary Road, Chesterton 46304; (219) 926–2255 or (800) 283–8687.

The magical kingdom of Oz is also a part of Dune Country. L. Frank Baum, author of the Oz books, used to summer here, and later his son established the International Wizard of Oz Club in this area. Today you can view a collection of Oz memorabilia in the ◆ **Wizard of Oz Museum,** housed in the Yellow Brick Road shop in Chesterton. The store is open 10:00 A.M. to 5:00 P.M. Monday through Saturday. It's easy to find: Just follow the yellow brick road (honestly!) to 109 East 950N, near 950N's intersection with State Road 49; (219) 926–7048. Each September a *Wizard of Oz* Festival, complete with several real-life Munchkins from the movie's original cast, evokes memories of the Judy Garland screen classic. Contact the Yellow Brick Road or the Porter County Convention, Recreation, and Visitors Commission (see previous entry).

The showpiece of Valparaiso in central Porter County is the striking ❖ **Chapel of the Resurrection** on the campus of Valparaiso University. This magnificent contemporary structure, which is the largest collegiate chapel in the nation, has received accolades from around the world. The entire building focuses on the chancel, whose limestone piers rise skyward for 98 feet and culminate in a roof shaped like a nine-point star. Try to visit here on a sunny day; from inside the chancel the view of the awe-inspiring stained-glass windows will take your breath away. The largest Lutheran university in the country, Valparaiso counts the late Lowell Thomas among its alumni. Visitors are welcome at any time; the campus lies at the east end of Union Street; (219) 464–5112.

Housed in a facility that simulates a medieval village, **Marc T. Nielsen Interiors, Inc.,** features crafts shops for upholstery work, cabinet making, and furniture building in a Tudor-style farm structure. There's also a display of Old World furniture and accessories that may be unlike any you've ever seen. Owner Virginia Phillips travels the world to buy antiques for the stunning collection. Store open 9:00 A.M. to 4:30 P.M. Monday through Friday; crafts shops by appointment. Located at 734 North Old Suman Road near Valparaiso; (219) 462–9812.

At the **Strongbow Turkey Inn** it's Thanksgiving all year long. You can have almost any part of the gobbler cooked nearly any way imaginable here. Turkey appears in salads, soups, sandwiches, crepes, pies, and pâtés, not to mention sliced up on a plate and accompanied by all the traditional fixings. Everything is made on the premises—breads, rolls, cranberry-orange relish, cakes, dessert pies, and a delicious cup custard. If you're in the mood for something continental, try the veal Oscar, Coquilles St. Jacques, or shrimp Pescatore. You'll find the inn at 2405 U.S. Highway 30 East, Valparaiso. Open 11:00 A.M. to 9:00 P.M. Sunday through Thursday; 11:00 A.M. to 10:00 P.M. Friday and Saturday; closed Christmas week. Reservations advised; (219) 462–5121. Stop at the Strongbow Bakery on the premises for some delectable take-home treats; (219) 464–8643.

St. Joseph County

If you ever wonder where all that spearmint in your Wrigley's chewing gum comes from, here's your chance to find out. Call the **Martin Blad Mint Farm** near South Bend and make an appointment to visit the place in July. That's when the bright yellow mint wagons haul a newly harvested crop into the mint-press building. You can watch as the oil is separated, picked up, guided through coils, and pumped into fifty-five-gallon containers. Then it's packed up and sent off to Wrigley's en masse. The 2,500-acre farm is located at 58995 State Road 123, ½ mile north of its junction with State Road 23, just southwest of South Bend; (219) 234-7271.

From nearly every vantage point in South Bend, you can see the renowned golden dome that tops the administration building of the ✦ **University of Notre Dame.** A walking tour of the 1,250-acre campus will take you to such places as the Grotto of Our Lady of Lourdes, an exact reproduction of the original in France; the Sacred Heart Church, an awe-inspiring Gothic structure that contains one of North America's oldest carillons; the Snite Museum of Art, which houses rare religious artworks and masterpieces by such noted artists as Chagall, Picasso, and Rodin; and the Notre Dame Memorial Library, a huge, fourteen-story building noted for its rare-books room and the 132-foot-high granite mural that adorns its outer wall. To reach the university go north from South Bend on U.S. Highway 31/33 to Angela Boulevard and turn east; call (219) 631-5000 for general information, 631-5726 for tour information.

Of all the citizens of South Bend, past or present, Knute Rockne is perhaps the best known. The famous coach, who maintained that football was a game of brains rather than brawn, shaped the Fighting Irish into a legend. When he died in a plane crash in 1931, he was just forty-two years old. His funeral service, attended by an estimated 100,000 people and carried by radio across the nation and to Norway (the land of his birth), was one of the most emotional in American history. You can visit his grave in **Highland Cemetery,** at 2557 Portage Avenue, not far from his beloved university.

Another name that's famous around South Bend is Studebaker. Clement Studebaker began his career as a wagon maker, making wagons for the Union Army during the Civil War and later for the thousands who trekked west. As he progressed from wagons to carriages to automobiles, he kept a collection of company vehicles. They are housed today in the ◆ **Studebaker National Museum** at 525 South Main Street. Among the exhibits is the Studebaker carriage in which Abraham Lincoln rode to Ford's Theatre the night he was assassinated. The museum is open from 9:00 A.M. to 5:00 P.M. Monday through Saturday and noon to 5:00 P.M. Sunday; closed holidays. Admission fee; (219) 235–9479 (information line), (219) 235–9108 (museum), or (219) 235–9714 (office).

By 1888 Studebaker had become a wealthy man, and he built himself a forty-room mansion worthy of his station, complete with twenty fireplaces and 24,000 square feet of space. Its massive stone walls, turrets, and irregular roofs gave it the appearance of a feudal castle. Today the historic mansion is called **Tippecanoe Place** and houses a fine gourmet restaurant that serves continental cuisine. Lunch is available from 11:30 A.M. to 2:00 P.M. Monday through Friday; dinner from 5:00 to 10:00 P.M. Monday through Thursday, 5:00 to 11:00 P.M. Friday, 4:30 to 11:00 P.M. Saturday, and 4:00 to 9:00 P.M. Sunday. A Sunday brunch is served buffet style from 9:00 A.M. to 2:00 P.M. Located at 620 West Washington Street; (219) 234–9077. Tours are available outside of dining hours. Reservations are advised for both meals and tours.

The only artificial white-water course in North America and one of only three in the world is located in the heart of downtown South Bend. Called the ◆ **East Race Waterway,** it's a 2,000-foot-long channel that bypasses the South Bend Dam across St. Joseph River. The elite of white-water paddlers from around the globe come here each summer to take part in national and international competitions. Because the flow of water can be controlled, the waterway can generate the churning rapids and 6-foot-tall waves needed for athletic events or can present a surface calm enough for whole families to embark on. It's open to the public for rafting, kayaking, and other water sports, under the watchful eyes of a well-trained rescue team, for approximately thirty hours per week throughout the summer; hours vary. The many adjacent walkways and bridges provide landlubbers with a close-up view of waterway happenings. Located east of St. Joseph River, along the west side of Niles Avenue and between Jefferson Boulevard on the south and Madison Street on the north. For additional information about competitive events, hours open to the public, and watercraft rental, contact the East Race Waterway and Recreation Corp., 126 North Niles Avenue, South Bend 46617; (219) 233–6121 or the South Bend Parks Department, 301 South St. Louis Boulevard, South Bend 46617; (219) 235–9401.

During spawning season the East Race Waterway also functions as a fish ladder, one of four such ladders on St. Joseph River. Steelhead trout and Chinook salmon are able to detour around four dams and travel freely along the 63-mile stretch of river between Mishawaka and Lake Michigan. Some 600,000 of those fish are reared annually at the **Richard Clay Bodine State Fish Hatchery** in Mishawaka. Visitors can take a free, self-guided tour of the facilities daily between 8:00 A.M. and 4:00 P.M. Monday through Friday and from 8:00 A.M. to noon Saturday and Sunday. Located at 13200 East Jefferson Boulevard; (219) 255–4199.

In Mishawaka the **100 Center Complex** of shops, restaurants, art galleries, and theaters occupies the original brick buildings of the Kamm & Schellinger Brewery (circa 1853). Located on the south bank of St. Joseph River at 700 Lincoln Way West; (219) 259–7861. The *Princess,* a stern-wheeler paddleboat that docks at the center, offers daily cruises between Mishawaka and South Bend from May through mid-October; (219) 259–6080.

Landscape architect Shoji Kanaoka went to Florida and designed the grounds at Epcot Center. He also came to Indiana and designed ❖ **Shiojiri Niwa,** a lovely 1.3-acre Japanese strolling garden located in the Merrifield Park Complex at 1000 East Mishawaka Avenue in Mishawaka. Among the garden's many pleasures are Oriental plantings, bridges, a tea garden, and dry waterfalls and streams. Visitors can sample its serenity at any hour of any day. Free admission; call (219) 258–1664.

TIPPECANOE COUNTY

On November 7, 1811, William Henry Harrison, then governor of the Indiana Territory, led his men in battle against the last all-Indian army to be assembled east of the Mississippi River. The Indians, representing a confederacy of tribes organized by Tecumseh and his brother, the Prophet, went down in defeat, ending any organized Indian resistance to the white man's settlement of the Northwest Territory. In later years Harrison's victory was a prominent factor in his successful bid for the presidency of the United States.

You can see an impressive 85-foot-tall monument and stroll the 96-acre grounds where the battle was actually fought at the ◆ **Tippecanoe Battlefield State Memorial** near the town of Battle Ground. A scenic trail leads past several trees that stood during the battle; musket balls are still found in the older trees when they fall. The park is also a peaceful and lovely spot for a picnic—except on those summer weekends when two noisy annual events take place. Dulcimers, guitars, mandolins, and more hold all-day, all-night jam sessions during the **Indiana Fiddler's Gathering;** less lyrical sounds fill the air when various types of old machinery rev up their motors at the **Antique Farm Power Show.** The park is open daily, free of charge, year-round during daylight hours. A museum on the grounds presents the history of the battle from both sides' points of view. Open 10:00 A.M. to 5:00 P.M. daily, March through November; 10:00 A.M. through 4:00 P.M. daily, December through February; closed winter holidays. Nominal admission fee. Located on Prophet's Rock Road just west of Battle Ground; follow signs; (317) 567–2147.

On certain nights, full moon or not, you can join a howling at Battle Ground's ◆ **Wolf Park.** The eerie but beautiful voices of the resident wolf pack drift through the air and send chills up and down your spine. If you like these misunderstood creatures, it is an experience you will never forget.

This unique wildlife park is a research facility, and you can visit during the day to watch scientists at work. Docents are on hand to tell you each wolf's name and rank order in the pack, and you can see the wolves interact with human beings whom the wolves have accepted as members of their "society." Each Sunday at 2:00 P.M., predators (wolves) and prey (bison) are placed together to demonstrate that a healthy animal has nothing to fear from wolves.

The park is operated by the nonprofit North American Wildlife Park Foundation, which charges a nominal admission fee to the park to help offset expenses. Advance reservations are required for the howls, generally held each Friday evening. The park is open 1:00 to 5:00 P.M. Saturday and Sunday from the first weekend in May to November 30; howls are held year-round. To reach the park go north from Battle Ground on Harrison Road for about 1 mile; Wolf Park signs point the way. Write Wolf Park, c/o North American Wildlife Park Foundation, RFD 1, Battle Ground 47920; (317) 567–2265.

In Lafayette the twenty-acre **Clegg Botanical Gardens** perch on the high bank of Wildcat Creek. Wander along a mile of marked trails that lead past ancient white oaks, sugar maples, and dogwoods. Daffodils bloom in the spring; hybrid daylilies unfold their petals in June and July, followed by resurrection lilies in August and Japanese anemones in September. From Lookout Point you can see the Indiana countryside for miles around. Open 10:00 A.M. to sunset daily; free. Located at 1782 North County Road 400 East; (317) 447–9999 or (800) 872–6648.

WHITE COUNTY

The small town of Brookston is home to the only professional handmade-paper mill in the country. Located at 300 East Third Street, the ◆ **Twinrocker Paper Mill** produces a wide variety of quality papers that range from nonsilver photography paper to archival paper to stationery and everything in between. Owners Kathryn and Howard Clark will design and produce any paper to any specifications a customer wants. Visitors can view the fascinating process from 8:00 A.M. to 5:00 P.M. Monday through Friday.

Twinrocker also sells papermaking supplies and offers workshops. For additional information contact Twinrocker Handmade Paper, P.O. Box 413, Brookston 47923; (317) 563–3119.

Before leaving Brookston, stop in at the **Klein Brot Haus,** a German bakery and cafe whose homemade breads are as unique as the papers made by its neighbor. Located at 106 East Third Street; (317) 563–3788.

SOUTHEAST INDIANA

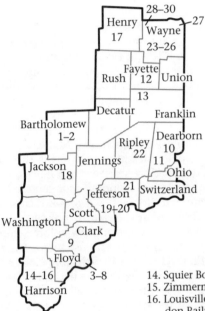

14. Squier Boone Caverns
15. Zimmerman Art Glass Factory
16. Louisville, New Albany & Cory-
    don Railroad
17. Indiana Basketball Hall of Fame
18. Muscatatuck National Wildlife
    Refuge
19. Lanier Mansion
20. Clifty Falls State Park
21. United National of the Poultry
    World
22. Tyson United Methodist Church
23. Hayes Regional Arboretum
24. Wayne County Historical
    Museum
25. Whitewater Gorge Park
26. Webb's Antique Mall
27. Levi Coffin House
28. Teetor House
29. Tedco, Inc.
30. Eagles in art

1. North Christian Church
2. Zaharako's Confectionery
3. Falls of the Ohio National
   Wildlife Conservation Area
4. Falls of the Ohio State Park
5. Jeffboat, Inc.
6. Howard Steamboat Museum
7. Slugger Park
8. Schimpff's Confectionery
9. Huber Orchard, Winery, and U-
   Pick Farm
10. Hillforest Mansion
11. Red Wolf Sanctuary
12. Whitewater Valley Railroad
13. Whitewater Canal State Historic
    Site

SOUTHEAST INDIANA
BARTHOLOMEW COUNTY

According to an article that appeared in the *New York Times Magazine* in recent years, "there is really no equivalent to Columbus anywhere." That's just one of many tributes this town of 31,000 people has received from around the world in recognition of its architecture. Fifty-five public and private buildings make up the most concentrated collection of contemporary architecture on earth, and the names of the architects, artists, designers, and sculptors who created them are right from the pages of *Who's Who*. Where else, for instance, can you walk out of a church designed by Eliel Saarinen, cross the street, pass a Henry Moore sculpture, and enter a library designed by I. M. Pei?

One of the most visually striking buildings is the ◆ **North Christian Church,** designed by Eero Saarinen (Eliel's son). A low, hexagon-shaped building, it has a sloping roof centered by a 192-foot-tall needlelike spire that's topped by a gold-leaf cross. The multilevels of **Smith Elementary School,** created by John M. Johansen, are connected by several brightly colored, tube-shaped ramps—pure delight for the children who use them. The new sanctuary of the **St. Paul's Lutheran Church,** topped by an 85-foot-tall, copper-clad steeple, rises in Byzantine-like splendor above its surroundings—beautiful at any time, especially so when touched by the sun. Just east of town the sprawling **Otter Creek Clubhouse** designed by Harry Weese lies adjacent to one of the finest public golf courses in the country; Robert Trent Jones, who laid out the course, says its thirteenth hole is the single best hole he's ever designed.

The beauty of the downtown area has recently been enhanced by a sprawling white structure that serves as the world headquarters of **Cummins Engine Company,** Columbus's oldest and leading firm. Outside, graceful fountains feed shallow ponds and fingers of vines meander up the walls. Inside, within the glassed-in lobby, a diesel engine—the product that first brought fame to the company—is displayed as an abstract sculpture. Since 1957, as part of its commitment to a quality environment for all town residents, the Cummins Foundation has paid the fees of all leading architects chosen by the town leaders, thus contributing to the overall design of the city itself.

North Christian Church

Not all of these buildings will knock the socks off you at first sight. To fully appreciate them you should learn something about the innovative functions and attention to details that lie behind the facades. Many will amaze you when you learn the years in which they were constructed; the **First Christian Church,** built in 1942, could just as easily have been built yesterday.

Columbus also has its share of renovations and historical buildings, but it is the modern architecture that has brought this small town fame as the "Athens of the Prairie."

Begin your tour at the Columbus Visitors Center, housed in a nineteenth-century home at 506 Fifth Street (812–372–1954), where you can pick up maps and descriptive cassette tapes for self-guided tours. Reservations can also be made in advance for a minibus guided tour, available daily April through October. The center is open 9:00 A.M. to 5:00 P.M. Monday through Saturday and 10:00 A.M. to 2:00 P.M. Sunday, April through October; hours vary the rest of the year. For additional information contact the Columbus Area Visitor Information Commission, P.O. Box 1477, Columbus 47202–1477; (812) 378–2622 or (800) 468–6564.

There's nothing contemporary about ✦ **Zaharako's Confectionery** in downtown Columbus—it's pure nostalgia. Located at the same address since October 1900, the store is now a Columbus institution. Its fixtures carry you back to the beginning of the century—Mexican onyx soda fountains purchased from the St. Louis World Exposition in 1905; a full-concert mechanical pipe organ brought here from Germany in 1908 that rings out with tunes of the Gay Nineties; an exquisite Tiffany lamp; and accessories of carved mahogany. Amid these ornate surroundings you can enjoy homemade ice cream, fountain treats, and an assortment of candy and sandwiches. You'll find the store at 329 Washington Street (812–379–9329), right across the street from Columbus's ultramodern, award-winning shopping mall and special events center, **The Commons,** designed by Cesar Pelli.

Completely enclosed, The Commons houses a unique playground that your children will want to take home with them. Also here is **Chaos I,** a seven-ton, 30-foot-tall, in-motion sculpture crafted out of scrap metal by Swiss artist Jean Tinguely; the piece becomes more intriguing the longer you look at it.

In 1895 the Romanesque Revival building at the corner of Fifth and Franklin streets was the brand-new Columbus City Hall.

Today it is an elegant bed-and-breakfast inn that ranks as one of the Midwest's finest. Meticulously renovated, the **Columbus Inn** combines the best of past and present. Each of the thirty rooms and five suites contains American Empire-style cherry furnishings—including beds that were custom-made in France—and some beautiful antiques. The efficiency kitchens in the suites boast microwave ovens, linen napkins, and French crystal. For breakfast guests are served such fare as an egg casserole (a unique dish that has contributed greatly to the inn's growing fame), fruit salad, homemade bread, and imported tea. Rates for two range from about $100 to $200 per night. For reservations write the inn at 445 Fifth Street, Columbus 47201, or call (812) 378–4289. Both guests and nonguests are invited to partake of afternoon tea from noon to 4:00 P.M., and high tea from 4:00 to 6:00 P.M.; prices range from $4.95 to $6.95.

CLARK COUNTY

Along the bank of the Ohio River in Clarksville lies a 400-million-year-old fossil bed that is one of the world's greatest natural wonders. Its rare and unusual formations date back to the Devonian age and have for decades attracted sightseers and scientists from around the world. Once the reef was covered by the Falls of the Ohio, a raging, 2-mile stretch of water below Louisville in which the Ohio River dropped 22 feet over limestone ledges. Now the Ohio has been reduced to a series of pools by a string of dams, and the controlled water levels have left the reef high and dry. Its fossil corals archaeological sites are among the best in the country, and the variety of its migratory bird life is unparalleled at any other inland location.

For years efforts have been underway to preserve this area. The first step in realizing that dream occurred in October 1984, when the U.S. Senate approved funding for the creation of the ❖ **Falls of the Ohio National Wildlife Conservation Area.** In 1990 sixty-eight acres of land were dedicated as Indiana's newest state park. Although relatively small itself, the ❖ **Falls of the Ohio State Park** lies within the 1,404 acres of the federally protected conservation area, providing lots of wide-open space to explore.

A 16,000-square-foot interpretive center, perched atop a bluff overlooking the fossil beds, opened to the public in January 1994.

The building's exterior features horizontal bands of Indiana limestone alternating with bands of earth-toned bricks, creating a layered look reminiscent of the geological treasure that sprawls below it.

Inside, exhibits lead visitors back through the millennia to a time when ancient Indiana lay about twenty degrees south of the equator beneath the warm waters of a tropical sea. An orientation video employs the latest laser technology to portray the history of the Falls. The use of underwater oceanic photography to re-create a 400-million-year-old tropical sea is a first in the film industry. In a wildlife observation room, human visitors can view some of the area's 265 species of avian visitors in a small garden area. Elsewhere, the center offers panoramic views of the Ohio River, a historic railroad bridge, the McAlpine Dam and Locks, and the fossil bed itself (best seen from August through October, when the river is at its lowest level).

Low-water periods also provide the best opportunity to explore the fossil bed. More than 600 fossil species have been identified here, and two-thirds of those were discovered here for the first time anywhere in the world. Visitors may walk among the eroded rock slabs and search for fossils freed from the bedrock by the powerful waters of the river. Handling of the fossils is encouraged, but they must be returned to their original locations. Collecting is strictly forbidden.

Other activities include fishing, picnicking, and hiking along park trails.

The park is located on the south side of Riverside Drive, about a mile west of U.S. 31. Admission is charged for both the park and the interpretive center, which are open 9:00 A.M. to 5:00 P.M. daily year-round. For additional information contact Falls of the Ohio State Park, 201 West Riverside Drive, Clarksville 47129; (812) 280–9970.

When you don't have any ocean waves close at hand, there's only one thing to do—create your own. And that's just what they've done at **Wave Tek Water Park** in Clarksville. In addition to the Olympic-size pool where 3-foot waves ripple the surface every few minutes, there's also the Rampage, a giant water roller coaster. Although it's part of the Marriott Inn Complex, the water park is open to the general public. Marriott Inn is located at 505 Marriott Drive; take the Stanisfer Avenue exit off I–65. The water park is open 10:00 A.M. to 6:00 P.M. daily, as well as 6:30 to 9:00 P.M. on Monday, Thursday, and Saturday, Memorial Day through Labor Day. Various admission fees depend on the facilities you use and how long you use them; (812) 282–8509.

Presiding over Clarksville is the town's own version of London's Big Ben. The main building of the Colgate-Palmolive plant at State and Woerner streets is topped by the **second-largest clock in the world,** which is a monstrous 40 feet in diameter and has a 16-foot-long hour hand that weighs 500 pounds. (The largest clock in the world, 50 feet in diameter, sits atop Colgate's plant in Jersey City, New Jersey.) No one in Clarksville gets away with saying he doesn't know the time—the electric-powered clock is reputed to be accurate to within fifteen seconds a month, the clock's face can be read from a distance of 2½ miles, and the clock is illuminated at night.

You can take a free tour of Colgate's facilities at 9:00 A.M. each Tuesday if you make an advance appointment; call Employee Relations at (812) 283–6611. The plant, which produces an array of household and personal-care products, is housed in a building that once served as Indiana's first state prison.

Jeffersonville, which adjoins Clarksville to the east, is home to the biggest inland boatbuilders in North America. You can see them at work along the waterfront building cruise ships, ferries, towboats, barges, and—with the impending arrival of riverboat gambling in Indiana—gaming boats. The company, known as ◆ **Jeffboat, Inc.,** has its offices at 1030 East Market Street; call (812) 288–0200 or 288–0400.

Each summer one of Jeffersonville's own comes home to visit. The *Mississippi Queen* passenger steamboat, built locally by Jeffboat, pauses here during its annual treks up and down the Ohio and Mississippi rivers. Her older sister, the *Delta Queen,* also stops here; both can be toured when they're tied up at the pier. Call 1–800–543–7637 for schedules and information.

Until 1931 the Howard Shipyards were in Jeffersonville. During their 107 years in business, the yards produced some 3,000 steamboats, reported to be the finest ever to ply the waters of North and Central America. The *J. M. White,* the most luxurious steamboat in history, was built here, as were the *Glendy Burke,* which inspired the Stephen Foster song of the same name; the *City of Louisville,* the fastest steamboat ever built; and the *Cape Girardeau,* captured

87

on film for all time in *Gone with the Wind.*

The steamboat era was flourishing in the 1890s when construction began on the elaborate twenty-two-room Howard mansion at 1101 East Market Street that today houses the ◆ **Howard Steamboat Museum.** A striking late-Victorian structure, the house features stained- and leaded-glass windows, a Moorish-style music room that contains its original née-Louis XV furniture, and intricate embellishments that were hand carved from fifteen types of wood.

You can see all this today, plus a priceless collection of relics that played a role in the golden era of steamboating, miniature models of Howard-built steamboats, and whole rooms furnished like staterooms on the finest turn-of-the-century boats. Open 10:00 A.M. to 3:00 P.M. Tuesday through Saturday and 1:00 to 3:00 P.M. Sunday; closed Monday and major holidays. Nominal admission fee. Write the Clark County Historical Society at P.O. Box 606, Jeffersonville 47130, or call (812) 283–3728 for further details.

Breathes there a man alive who never to himself has said (at least in the days of his youth), "Boy, would I love to have a Louisville Slugger!" One would think, of course, that they're made in Louisville, but such is not the case. The world-famous hardwood bats, some one million of them each year, are manufactured at the ◆ **Hillerich and Bradsby Company** plant in Jeffersonville.

Most are shaped on semiautomatic lathes, but those used by professional baseball players are still hand turned by the most skilled of craftsmen. According to a company executive, the custom-made models are necessary because a pro can tell the difference of a fraction of an ounce in weight or of a sixteenth of an inch in the handle size. During the free tour you'll even receive a miniature (18-inch-long) Louisville Slugger to commemorate your visit.

Die-hard baseball fans will especially enjoy the company's **Bat Museum,** which contains Sluggers used by the most famous players in history. One was used by Ty Cobb during his last week in the majors. Another used by Babe Ruth to hit twenty-one home runs, and he personally notched his bat for each one. You'll also see bats once swung by such notables as Pete Rose, Stan Musial, Hank Aaron, and Lou Gehrig.

The museum is open 8:00 A.M. to noon and 1:00 to 3:30 P.M. Monday through Friday; plant tours are generally conducted at 9:00 A.M., 10:00 A.M., 1:00 P.M., and 2:00 P.M. Monday through Friday; the plant is closed the last three workdays in June, the first two weeks in July, national holidays, and Christmas week. For exact tour times call (502) 585–5226, extension 201 (at the company's headquarters just across the Ohio River in Louisville, Kentucky). The plant, known as ◆ **Slugger Park,** also produces PowerBilt golf clubs. Located at 1525 Charlestown-New Albany Road, just off Interstate 65 at the Cementville/Clarksville exit.

In 1991 ◆ **Schimpff's Confectionery** at 347 Spring Street celebrated its one-hundredth birthday. An old-fashioned candy store complete with soda fountain and tin ceiling, Schimpff's is one of the oldest continuously family-owned candy businesses in the country. Its cinnamon red-hot squares are a particular favorite, ordered through the mail by people all over the country and even in a few foreign countries. The folks in Bakersfield, California, for example, order sixty to eighty pounds of red hots annually. All candies are handmade, just as they were a century ago. They're all scrumptious, and the ice cream's good, too! Open 10:00 A.M. to 5:00 P.M. Monday through Friday and 10:00 A.M. to 3:00 P.M. Saturday; (812) 283–8367.

Something's always going on at the 550-acre Huber Farm near Borden. Officially billed as the ◆ **Huber Orchard, Winery, and U-Pick Farm,** it's open to the public year-round. Strawberries are ripe for the picking from mid-May through mid-June. Twelve varieties of apples are in season from late summer through December. You can select your own pumpkin right from the patch in the fall and cut your own Christmas tree in December. Cider made on the farm each fall is available for purchase at any time.

Brothers Gerald and Carl Huber, along with their families, have turned their talents to commercial winemaking in recent years, and thus far they've garnered more than fifty awards for their efforts, including "Best of Show" at the 1983 Indiana State Fair and a silver medal at the prestigious Eastern International Wine Competition in 1991. Visitors can sample their eighteen varieties and tour the winery. The Hubers also make cheese on their farm, and visitors can watch this process as well. You can buy the makings of a picnic lunch, as well as ready-made sandwiches and cheese trays, right on the farm. The winery, the cheese factory, and a gift shop are open Tuesday through Sunday year-round, but hours vary. Call (812) 923–9813 or 923–9463 for hours and exact directions, or write the Hubers at 19816 Huber Road, Borden 47106.

Just down the road, on a 360-acre farm, cousin Joe runs the **Joe Huber Family Restaurant.** The down-home country cooking, which features fried chicken, fried biscuits, and fresh fruit and vegetables, is served family style. Open 11:00 A.M. to 8:00 P.M. Monday through Thursday, 11:00 A.M. to 10:00 P.M. Friday and Saturday, and 11:00 A.M. to 6:00 P.M. Sunday, March through December. Located at 2421 Scottsville Road; (812) 923–5255.

DEARBORN COUNTY

Atop a wooded hillside overlooking the village of Aurora stands a splendid yellow frame house filled with the memories of a bygone era. It was built in the 1850s by Thomas Gaff, a wealthy industrialist and shipping magnate whose steamboats regularly plied the waters of the Ohio River far below.

Gaff's love for the river ran deep, and that love is reflected in his home, ◆ **Hillforest Mansion,** whose architectural style is often referred to as "steamboat Gothic." And indeed it does resemble a steamboat in part, with its rounded front porticoes and cupola, coupled columns, and suspended interior staircase—all features that were typical of the "floating palaces" that graced our country's rivers in the heyday of river transportation.

Now restored and filled with antique furniture, the entire mansion can be toured, from its wine cellar up to the observatory at the top of the house. The view of the Ohio River is just as beautiful as it was when Thomas Gaff himself stood here. Around the one-of-a-kind home are ten acres of grounds laid out in the grand manner of an Italian villa. Open 1:00 to 5:00 P.M. Tuesday through Sunday, April through December 23; admission fee; situated at 213 Fifth Street; (812) 926–0087.

About 2½ miles west of Aurora on U.S. Highway 50, you'll find an attractive restaurant built around a living tree; it's called, appropriately enough, **The Tree House.** Hanging plants, brick archways, and a glass roof contribute to the garden atmosphere. Specialties of the house include barbecued ribs, veal parmesan, seafood, filet mignon, and prime rib, which, at dinnertime, will cost you from about $11 to $20. Buffets are offered Friday night and Sunday. Children's menus available; reservations recommended. Open 11:00 A.M. to 9:00 P.M. Tuesday through Thursday, 11:00 A.M. to 10:00 P.M. Friday and Saturday, 11:00 A.M. to 8:00 P.M. Sunday, closed Monday, January 1–17 and December 25; (812) 926–3737.

Named for an animal now extinct in the wild, the ◆ **Red Wolf Sanctuary** near Dillsboro is home to several red and gray wolves, coyotes, foxes, a mountain lion, and an assortment of raptors. The red wolves seen here are hybrids (part coyote)—the few remaining pure red wolves in this country live on lands managed by the U.S. Fish and Wildlife Service.

Established more than ten years ago by Paul Strasser, a former zookeeper, the twenty-three-acre refuge also serves as a rehabilitation center for sick and injured wildlife from all over the country. Paul and his wife, Jane, nurse their wild charges back to health, returning those who fully recuperate to their natural habitats and adding the others to their growing "family."

The Strassers welcome visitors to their sanctuary free of charge from Thursday through Sunday year-round, but they request that you call in advance and make an appointment. If you want to see the newborn young, come in the spring. Located approximately 5 miles southwest of Dillsboro via State Road 62. Contact the sanctuary at P.O. Box 23, Dillsboro 47018; (812) 667–5303.

DECATUR COUNTY

It's easy to tell the visitors from the hometown folks in Greensburg—the visitors are all looking up. Up, that is, at a tree that's growing where we've all been led to believe trees can't grow—on a roof. Eye-catching, to be sure.

The tree adorns the tower that tops the Decatur County Courthouse. When the first tree appeared here in 1870, local authorities, who knew a tree's proper place, grubbed it out. Five years later a second tree appeared. The amazed citizenry, admiring its tenacity, merely stood by and watched this time. That tree thrived until 1929, when it failed to leaf and was removed to the local **Decatur County Museum** for preservation.

At the time of its removal another tree had already started

growing on the opposite side of the tower. It was later joined by a second tree, so that today there are actually two trees, both growing without any apparent nourishment (although local comedians conjecture that they are fed by the springs in the tower's clock). The townsfolk have long since made their peace with this peculiar situation, and they even celebrate each September with a **Tree City Fall Festival.**

What type of tree had implanted itself on the courthouse roof? For years no one could agree on the answer, and finally scientists at the Smithsonian Institution in Washington, D.C., were consulted. They declared the trees to be large-toothed aspens. For additional information contact the Greensburg Area Chamber of Commerce, 125 West Main Street, Greensburg 47240; (812) 663–2832.

FAYETTE COUNTY

The ❖ **Whitewater Valley Railroad,** the longest steam railroad in Indiana, travels 32 scenic miles between Connersville and Metamora (see Franklin County) each Saturday, Sunday, and holiday from May through November. All the sights and sounds of old-time steam travel have been re-created to transport you back in time, and places of interest, including some of the original canal locks, are pointed out along the way. Two rare Baldwin locomotives, vintage 1907 and 1919, pull New York Central and Erie Stillwell passenger cars over tracks laid along the towpath of the old Whitewater Canal. At Metamora there's time to disembark and explore a restored canal town.

Both round-trips and one-way trips, as well as caboose rides and special Christmas runs, are available. Round-trips, which are approximately five hours long, originate at the Connersville station, located 1 mile south of town on State Road 121. Write the Whitewater Valley Railroad, Inc., P.O. Box 406, Connersville 47331; call (317) 825–2054 in Connersville or (317) 647–3162 in Metamora.

Seven miles southwest of Connersville on County Road 350S is the **Mary Gray Bird Sanctuary,** a 684-acre wildlife preserve owned and operated by the Indiana Audubon Society. These peaceful surroundings are crisscrossed by several miles of hiking trails, and a full-time naturalist is on hand to answer your ques-

Whitewater Valley Railroad

tions. A small museum depicts local flora and fauna. The preserve is open daily, free of charge, from dawn to dusk. Contact the sanctuary at RR 6, Box 165, Connersville 47331; (317) 827–0908.

FRANKLIN COUNTY

Not too long ago, Metamora was a dying town, its days numbered by the end of the canal era. That was before the state of Indiana decided to restore a 14-mile section of the old ◆ **Whitewater Canal,** originally a 76-mile waterway constructed in the mid-1800s, and now the small village hums with activity.

An 80-foot-long covered wooden aqueduct in Metamora was built in 1848 to carry the canal 16 feet above Duck Creek. Believed to be the only such structure in existence, it was once featured in *Ripley's Believe It or Not.*

A horse-drawn canal boat takes visitors for a leisurely 30-minute cruise through the aqueduct and a restored lock. Occasionally the Whitewater Valley Railroad's steam train chugs by carrying passengers between its Connersville station and Metamora (see Fayette County).

Many of the town's fine arts, crafts, and specialty shops are housed in pre–Civil War buildings that cling to the banks of the canal; others occupy reconstructed and reproduced buildings elsewhere in a section known as Old Metamora. An aged brick gristmill still grinds and sells flour, cornmeal, and grits. The total effect is that of a country village suspended in the 1830s.

Of the many special events scheduled throughout the year, the loveliest is the Christmas Walk that's held evenings on the first three Fridays and Saturdays after Thanksgiving. Some 3,000 luminaries line the banks of the canal, roads, and walkways. Carolers stroll through the streets; horses clippity-clop along, pulling carriages behind them. The aroma of hot spiced cider perfumes the air. Quite a show for a town that has a population of about sixty permanent residents!

If while in Metamora you experience a bit of déjà vu, it may be because you've seen the movie *Rain Man.* Dustin Hoffman and Tom Cruise came here to shoot part of the film, which won the Academy Award for Best Picture of the Year in 1988.

Most shops are open 10:00 A.M. to 5:00 P.M. Tuesday through Friday and 9:00 A.M. to 6:00 P.M. Saturday, Sunday, and holidays, from mid-April to mid-December, while some are open only on weekends. Head for the shops flying bright yellow flags; that's Metamoraese for "Come on in! We're open!" For additional information contact the Metamora Visitor Center, P.O. Box 117, Metamora 47030; (317) 647–2109.

The canal boat operates on the hour from noon to 3:00 P.M. Wednesday through Friday and 11:00 A.M. to 4:00 P.M. Saturday and Sunday, May through October (by reservation only on May weekdays); a nominal fee is charged. Contact the Whitewater Canal State Memorial, P.O. Box 88, Metamora 47030; (317) 647–6512.

Oldenburg is another architectural and historical gem that has dwelt in the past century since it was founded in 1837. Known as the **"Village of Spires"** because of its many soaring steeples, Oldenburg is the home of the ◆ **convent and academy of the Sisters of St. Francis,** an order that originally came here from

Austria. The peaceful grounds, which invite leisurely strolls, include a cemetery reserved for the Sisters. In warm-weather months the cemetery is a stunning mosaic in green and white—paths edged by low-cut green hedges, emerald lawns shaded by the sprawling branches of ancient shade trees, and row on row of small, white, identical stone crosses. The convent itself, renowned for its ceiling frescoes, basilica-like chapel, iron stairways, and solid oak woodwork, can be toured by appointment. Call (812) 934-2475.

Elsewhere in the picturesque community are houses and storefronts adorned with the ornate tinwork of master craftsman Gasper Gaupel. The lovely tree-lined streets bear German names, ranging from the mundane Haupstrasse (Main Street) to the lyrical Schweineschwantz Gasse (Pigtail Alley). Every so often the aroma of brats and sauerkraut escapes from a local eatery. If you'd like to sample some German cuisine, just follow your nose.

HARRISON COUNTY

A few miles south of Corydon is a peaceful valley laced with subterranean caverns and edged by forested hills. Squire Boone first saw this area in the late 1700s while hunting with his older brother, Daniel, and eventually returned here to settle down, building a home for his family and a gristmill that provided their means of support. When he died in 1815 he was buried at his own request in the cave that today bears his name, and the walnut coffin that contains his remains can be seen on a guided tour.

◆ **Squire Boone Caverns** offer a wondrous mix of colorful stalactites and stalagmites, underground streams, waterfalls, twisted helictites, massive pillars of stone, and the world's largest travertine dam formation. Cave crickets, blind crayfish, isopods, amphipods, and a few bats live in the cave's deepest recesses. The tour guides are extremely well informed about this cave and about caves in general. At one point along the way, in the belly of the cave, all lights are turned out—an eerie experience that gives new meaning to the word *black*. This is not the largest cave around, but it is certainly one of the most dazzling. Visitors should be aware that the subterranean temperature is a constant fifty-four degrees, and there is a steep spiral staircase to climb at the end of the fifty-five minute, ⅓-mile tour.

Topside, you can visit an operating gristmill rebuilt on the original foundation used by Squire Boone, watch the miller at work, and buy his products. A cluster of log cabins near the cave's entrance houses various crafts shops, an art gallery, a homemade-candy store, and a restaurant; the craftspeople who work here are as authentic as the log cabins that shelter them. Children can get acquainted with farm animals at a petting zoo.

Although it's small in size and limited in menu, the restaurant serves some of the finest homemade soups, sandwiches, salads, and desserts in southern Indiana. Even the coffee and iced tea are exceptional, and the restaurant itself is bright, airy, clean, and cheerful.

To reach Squire Boone Caverns and Village, go south from Corydon on State Road 135 for about 10 miles, then turn east on Squire Boone Caverns Road for another 3 miles; look for signs. Cave tours start daily every thirty minutes from 10:00 A.M. to 6:00 P.M., Memorial Day weekend through Labor Day; village activities from 10:00 A.M. to 6:00 P.M. daily from Memorial Day weekend through August 20, Saturday and Sunday from August 21 through Labor Day. Cave tours only (at 10:00 A.M., noon, 2:00 P.M., and 4:00 P.M.) the rest of the year; closed major winter holidays. The gristmill, which lies just outside the cave-village complex, is open, free of charge, when the village is open. Write P.O. Box 411, Corydon 47112; or call (812) 732–4381 or (502) 425–2283.

Back in Corydon at the ◆ **Zimmerman Art Glass Factory** you can observe a process that is now nearly extinct. Brothers Bart and Kerry Zimmerman hand-blow every piece of glassware they make, and no two pieces are identical. The Zimmermans specialize in paperweights—clear crystal balls, large and small, that enclose unfolding blossoms—but will try just about anything that tickles their fancy. Their glass menagerie includes trays of glass fruits, sugar bowls and creamers, an assortment of baskets, lamps, vases, and perfume decanters—some clear, some in exquisite color.

Many customers order items made to their specifications. An example is the lady from Australia who dropped by to describe the lamp she wanted and asked the partners to send it to her home— the shipping charges cost more than the lamp.

Although small, the company is nationally known, and its artistic wares are displayed in many museums, including the Smithsonian Institution. You're welcome to drop in and watch these skilled craftsmen breathe life into molten glass; free glass-sculpting demonstrations are given from 9:00 A.M. to 3:00 P.M. Tuesday through Friday. The factory, open from 8:00 A.M. to 4:00 P.M. Tuesday through Saturday except major holidays, is housed in a green, corrugated-metal shed at 395 Valley Road NW, right next to the Hudson Foods poultry-processing plant on the south edge of Corydon; (812) 738–2206.

The ◆ **Louisville, New Albany & Corydon Railroad** is one of the shortest railroads in the nation—its entire track is just under 8 miles in length. Established in 1883, "The Dinky," as it's affectionately known to local residents, has been hauling freight from Corydon to Corydon Junction ever since. Railroad enthusiasts can accompany the engineer and crew on a 16-mile round-trip by special arrangement. The depot at Walnut and Water streets in Corydon displays antique railroad equipment; (812) 738–3171. Each weekend from spring through fall the **Corydon 1883 Scenic Railroad** embarks from the depot on 1½-hour round-trip tours through Southern Indiana hill country. For additional information contact the railroad at the LNAC Railroad Station, 210 Walnut Street NE, Corydon 47112; (812) 738–8000.

HENRY COUNTY

In Indiana it's known as "Hoosier Hysteria"; to the rest of the world it's known as basketball. Almost anyone, after spending about five minutes in Indiana, can tell you that basketball holds a special place in the hearts of Hoosiers. It is not unheard of, for instance, for whole towns—gas stations, restaurants, and shops included—to shut down totally so that everyone can go to the local high-school basketball game. After a short visit to the state, CBS news anchor Dan Rather was heard to remark that "a ball and a net would make a perfect state flag" for Indiana. The world's record attendance for an indoor basketball game occurred in 1984, when 67,596 persons attended an exhibition game between the National Basketball Association All Stars and the U.S. Olympic team in Indianapolis. In 1990 two Indiana teams playing for the state championship set a national record for attendance at a high-school basketball game—41,046 persons showed up to cheer on their favorites. Eighteen of the twenty largest high-school gyms in the country are in Indiana.

It should therefore surprise no one that there is an ◆ **Indiana**

Basketball Hall of Fame; the citizenry would have it no other way. Previously located in Indianapolis, the Hall of Fame moved to newer and roomier quarters in New Castle in 1990. Within its walls visitors can see multimedia presentations, use computers to research the basketball history of state schools, play a trivia game, try to outwit a mechanical guard, have the opportunity to make the winning shot as a clock counts down the last five seconds of a game, and learn basketball lore in abundance. The museum stands, appropriately, next door to the New Castle High School gym—the largest high-school gym in the world. Located at One Hall of Fame Court; nominal admission fee. Open 10:00 A.M. to 5:00 P.M. Tuesday through Saturday and noon to 5:00 P.M. Sunday; closed major winter holidays; (317) 529–1891.

JACKSON COUNTY

The heavenly aroma that sometimes tantalizes the nostrils in Brownstown is a vanilla bean on its way to becoming vanilla extract. This metamorphosis takes place each working day at the **Marion-Kay Spice Company** plant, which turns out an array of spices and seasonings. You can learn about the whole process, as well as the history of spices, on a free tour. The Marion-Kay plant is located at 1351 West U.S. Highway 50 on the western edge of town. Open 8:00 A.M. to 4:30 P.M. Monday through Friday; call (812) 358–3000 for tour hours.

Indiana's **Skyline Drive** meanders across a series of knobs for some 6 miles through the **Jackson-Washington State Forest** and offers spectacular hilltop vistas. The poorly surfaced road is hilly and treacherous, so plan on taking your time. To reach the drive, head south from Brownstown on South Poplar Street and follow the signs. Write the Jackson-Washington State Forest, 1278 East State Road 250, Brownstown 47220, or call (812) 358–2160, for information about the drive and the many recreational opportunities elsewhere in the forest.

Jackson County has the finest collection of long covered bridges in the state. Three of them span the East Fork of White River. To view what's billed as one of the longest covered bridges in the world, head east from Medora for 1 mile on State Road 235. The 434-foot-long span, built in 1875, is certainly the longest in Indiana. It carried traffic across the river until 1974, when it was bypassed by a new bridge. Sadly, the old **Medora Bridge** is slowly falling into decay—the cost to preserve it has thus far been out of reach.

The 325-foot-long **Bell's Ford Bridge** is the only triple-burr-arch covered bridge in Indiana and the only known Post truss bridge in existence anywhere. Erected in 1869, the Post truss represents a period when bridges were evolving from all-wood into all-metal or concrete structures. Its sides and floor feature iron rods and straps covered with wood. Located on State Road 258, 3 miles west of Seymour.

The **Shieldstown Covered Bridge,** constructed in 1876, is 331 feet long. To visit it go southwest from Seymour on U.S. Highway 50 for about 6½ miles, then turn northwest onto a country road leading to Crane Hill and proceed about 1 mile; look for signs along the way.

For additional information about the county's bridges, contact the Greater Seymour Chamber of Commerce, 105 South Chestnut Street, P.O. Box 312, Seymour 47274; (812) 522–3681.

Wildlife lovers will want to stop at ✦ **Muscatatuck National Wildlife Refuge,** located 3 miles east of Seymour on the south side of Highway 50. Covering more than 7,700 acres, it's Indiana's only such refuge and was established primarily as a sanctuary for wood ducks. Each spring and fall thousands of migrating waterfowl pause to rest on the open water and are occasionally joined by flocks of sandhill cranes. White-tailed deer and wild turkeys make their homes here all year long. The refuge is open daily year-round, from dawn to dusk; nominal admission fee. Contact the Muscatatuck National Wildlife Refuge, Route 7, Box 189A, Seymour 47274; (812) 522–4352.

JEFFERSON COUNTY

Charles Kuralt once called Madison the most beautiful river town in America. The curator of a Michigan museum, when he first saw Madison, said, "Put a fence around the entire town and don't let anyone touch anything in it!" During World War II the Office of War Information selected Madison as the "typical American town" and made movies of it in thirty-two languages to distribute around the world and to remind our troops what they were fighting for. *Life* magazine chose Madison as the most pleasant small town in the country in which to live. Its nineteenth-century archi-tecture, a mix of several styles, has been praised as the most beau-tiful in the Midwest, and its setting on the banks of the Ohio River, against a backdrop of wooded hills and limestone bluffs, is equally lovely. Obviously if you're going to tour Indiana, Madison is one place you shouldn't miss.

Once Madison was a thriving river port and the largest town in the state. When railroads arrived on the scene, the river traffic departed, and Madison, in keeping with the times, built its own railroad. What no one foresaw was that nearly everyone would get on the train and leave town. For many years no one came to replace the populace that had moved on, and 133 blocks of build-ings thus survived an era when it was fashionable to tear down anything old and replace it with something new in the name of progress. It is this legacy of architectural splendor that can be seen today.

The most notable building is the ◆ **Lanier Mansion** at 511 West First Street, a palatial home built in the 1840s for about $50,000—quite a chunk of money in those days. Its owner, James Lanier, was an astute banker whose loans to the state government during the Civil War helped Indiana avert bankruptcy. Facing a broad lawn that rambles down to the Ohio River, the Lanier Man-sion is an outstanding example of the Greek Revival style. Its two-story portico is supported by tall Corinthian columns and hemmed in by wrought-iron grillwork. Inside, a spiral staircase climbs three stories, unsupported except by its own thrust, and each of the rooms is decorated with period furniture and acces-sories. Now a state memorial, the five-acre estate is open free of charge year-round. Hours are 9:00 A.M. to 5:00 P.M. Wednesday through Saturday and 1:00 to 5:00 P.M. on Tuesday and Sunday; closed Monday, Thanksgiving, and Christmas; (812) 265–3526.

Among the other attractions in Madison's historic district are the office and private hospital of Dr. William Hutchings, with all the original medications and possessions of the late-nineteenth-century doctor still intact; a restored pioneer garden with vintage roses and other period plantings; and the Francis Costigan House, home of the architect who designed Lanier Mansion. Everywhere in Madison you'll see elaborate ornamental ironwork reminiscent of New Orleans but forged locally (as was much of New Orleans's ironwork). "Little Jimmy," a locally famous weathervane, sits atop the firehouse bell tower.

If the *Delta Queen,* an old stern-wheeler that carries passengers on nostalgic journeys up and down the Ohio and Mississippi rivers, happens to be in port during your visit, the aura of yesteryear will be even more overwhelming. The majestic old boat can be toured when it's docked.

Maps and guides for walking tours are available from the Madison Area Convention and Visitors Bureau at 301 East Main Street, just across the street from the Jefferson County Courthouse; (812) 265–2956 or 1–800–559–2956.

Railroad buffs will want to take a look at one of the world's steepest noncog train tracks. Cut through limestone bluffs in 1835, it climbs 413 feet in little more than a mile. Eight-horse teams drew the first trains up the incline but were eventually replaced by a wood-burning steam engine. The tracks can be viewed from State Road 56 at the west edge of town.

Madison is located in the heart of burley tobacco country, and each year from about Thanksgiving through January, auctions are conducted in local **tobacco warehouses.** It's a fascinating scenario, set to the music of the auctioneer's lyrical but unintelligible (to the layman) lingo. Two warehouses welcome visitors: Ford, 748 Scott Court, (812) 265–4061; and Morrow, 740 Clifty Drive, (812) 273–3610. Check locally for varying hours.

Not far west of Madison you can stay at the **Clifty Falls State Park Inn.** Recently renovated, it features guest rooms for $42 to $49 per night for two; some rooms have private balconies that overlook the Ohio River valley. The dining room serves three meals a day for reasonable rates. Write Clifty Inn, Box 387, Madison 47250; (812) 265–4135.

Noted for its natural beauty, ◈ **Clifty Falls State Park** sprawls over 1,360 hilly acres. The prettiest area, **Clifty Canyon State Nature Preserve,** is accessible only on foot. The great boulder-strewn canyon is so deep that sunlight can penetrate it only at high noon. Mosses, lichens, and ferns cling to the precipitous cliffs along Clifty Creek. In the spring, when the water is running fast, there are spectacular waterfalls; Big Clifty Falls, the granddaddy of them all, drops 60 feet. The park also offers an Olympic-size swimming pool, a modern campground, a nature center, an exercise trail, and breathtaking views from atop a 400-foot bluff. Contact Clifty Falls State Park, 1501 Green Road, Madison 47250; (812) 265–1331.

Canaan is a really fowl place. In fact there may be more fowl than people—and of more types than you ever knew existed. Schoolteacher Gale Ferris calls his poultry farm the ♦ **United Nations of the Poultry World.** Forty rare breeds populate his farmyard, including silver spangled hamburgs from Germany, black cochin bantams from Asia, bearded mottled houdans from France, and the blue-skinned Chinese silkies, as fluffy as powder puffs. The unusual araucanas from South America actually lay colored eggs.

Mr. Ferris is happy to share his wealth of knowledge—both about fowls and about Jefferson County. Early April, when all the redbuds are in bloom and baby chicks and ducks are about, is the recommended time. From mid-November to mid-April it's best to come on weekends or evenings. There is no charge, but donations are appreciated. To make sure Mr. Ferris will be there when you visit or to arrange group tours, call (812) 839–4770. The Ferris farm is located 15 miles northeast of Madison and 3 miles east of Canaan on State Road 62.

Also on the Ferris farm, housed in a little red barn, is a display of old tools and utensils dating from the early 1800s to the early 1900s, including a copper kettle, liquor jugs more than one hundred years old, and dippers for molten bullet metal. Nearby stands a miniature one-room schoolhouse that the Ferris family built from brick. It contains several pieces from an old Canaan school that was razed a few years back, including the cornerstone, coal tongs, blackboard, and school bench; other items on display are authentic antiques. Both attractions are open to the public free of charge.

Mr. Ferris is also one of the chief organizers of Canaan's annual Fall Festival, which features a potpourri of such events as a frog-jumping contest, a bucksaw woodcutting contest, a greased-pole climbing contest, and the Chief White Eye painting contest. Held the second weekend in September, the festival has become known far and wide, however, for its unique Pony Express Run. Mail is specially stamped at Canaan, packed in authentic Pony Express mailbags on loan from the Smithsonian Institution in Washington, D.C., and delivered to the Madison post office by a rider on horseback. For further information contact Mr. Ferris at 9713 North State Road 62, Canaan 47224; (812) 839–4770.

RIPLEY COUNTY

Many a visitor, while traveling through the small town of Versailles, has stopped to stare in wonderment at the unusual-looking church on the corner of Tyson and Adams streets. Known officially as the ✦ **Tyson United Methodist Church** and unofficially as the Tyson Temple, it is a continuous flow of rounded corners, arches, columns, windows, and roof. Its striking spire is a rounded, inverted cone of openwork aluminum. Inside, the altar is framed by columns that duplicate those in the Taj Mahal. The rounded ceiling above the pews is painted with the stars and constellations that appear over Indiana in October. To enhance the effect of a nighttime sky, the ceiling is illuminated by light reflected from wall fixtures. The dome over the choir loft is covered with gold leaf from Germany. Pulpit furnishings come from Italy, and the windows are from Belgium. The grand but small Tyson Church (it seats only 200 people) draws visitors from all over the nation. Free tours are offered by appointment; call (812) 689–6976 or 689–5046.

In Batesville you can enter the Old World atmosphere of the **Sherman House** and enjoy some of the tastiest food in southern Indiana. Diners can select one of twenty moderately priced entrées or the specialty of the day, but fresh Maine lobster from the restaurant's tank, chateaubriand, veal cordon bleu, prime strip steaks, and Hoosier-fried chicken are among the longtime favorites. The Sherman House also offers overnight accommodations at a rate of $40 to $55 for two. Although the inn has undergone several renovations since opening in 1852, the 30-inch-square, 90-foot-long yellow poplar timbers used in the original structure are still in place and still in perfect condition. Restaurant open 6:30 A.M. to 8:45 P.M. Monday through Thursday, 6:30 A.M. to 9:45 P.M. Friday and Saturday, and 6:30 A.M. to 7:45 P.M. Sunday; closed Christmas and New Year's; reservations recommended. Located at 35 South Main Street (State Road 229); (812) 934–2407.

WAYNE COUNTY

Although it may seem an unlikely location for such an enterprise, Richmond boasts one of the largest rose-growing industries in the world. **Hill Floral Products, Inc.,** pioneers in greenhouse rose growing since 1881, annually ships more than thirty million cut roses to midwestern and southern states. The famed American Beauty Rose was developed here, and new hybrids continue to be produced each year. Free tours are conducted during the annual Richmond Area Rose Festival each June; free tours for groups of ten or more year-round by appointment. Located at 2117 Peacock Road; call (317) 935–8687 or 1–800–828–8414.

The luxurious **Hill Memorial Rose Garden** in Glen Miller Park, which displays more than 1,600 rosebushes, was established in tribute to the local flower industry. Located at 2200 National Road East, the park is also the site of a small zoo. Park open 6:00 A.M. to 11:00 P.M. daily; (317) 935–8687.

At the ◆ **Hayes Regional Arboretum,** a 355-acre botanical preserve, you can view regional plant species—all labeled—on a 3½-mile auto tour. Also on the grounds are Indiana's first solar-heated greenhouse, a fern garden, a wild bird sanctuary, 10 miles of hiking trails (one of which passes an Indian mound), and a nature center housed in a barn some 180 years old, where a telephone line permits you to eavesdrop on a colony of bees busily at work making honey. The arboretum is open 9:00 A.M. to 5:00 P.M. Tuesday through Saturday and 1:00 to 5:00 P.M. Sunday, year-round. The nature center is open 9:00 A.M. to 5:00 P.M. Tuesday through Saturday and 1:00 to 5:00 P.M. Sunday, April through November; arboretum closed major winter holidays. Free admission. Contact the Hayes Regional Arboretum, 801 Elks Country Club Road, Richmond 47374; (317) 962–3745.

Following a disastrous gas explosion and fire in 1968 that destroyed much of the downtown business district, Richmond covered its physical scars by building an unusual **Downtown Promenade.** The 5 blocks of flowing fountains, soft music, and unique specialty stores have been nationally acclaimed for their beauty. You'll find the promenade on Main Street between Fifth and Tenth streets; (317) 962–8151.

The ◆ **Wayne County Historical Museum,** not far from the promenade area, is generally recognized as one of the best county museums in the state. Its diverse collection ranges from vintage cars made in Richmond to a Japanese samurai warrior's uniform, from a nineteenth-century general store to a 3,000-year-old mummy (X rays of the mummy taken by two local physicians can be seen by visitors). Open 9:00 A.M. to 4:00 P.M. Tuesday through Friday and 1:00 to 4:00 P.M. Saturday and Sunday, early February through mid-December; closed the rest of the year and major holidays. Nominal admission fee. Contact Wayne County Historical Museum, 1150 North A Street, Richmond 47374; (317) 962–5756.

Although every other sport takes a backseat to basketball in Indiana, the state has also produced some football heroes. They're all honored in the **Indiana Football Hall of Fame,** located at 815 North A Street. Among the inductees are O. J. Simpson, Bart Starr, and Jim Thorpe, all of whom once played football in the Hoosier State; Knute Rockne, the legendary coach of Notre Dame; and Weeb Ewbank, a local great who coached the Baltimore Colts and New York Jets. Tony Hulman, whose name is synonymous with the Indianapolis 500, is remembered here as an All-American end on the undefeated Yale University team of 1923. Open Monday through Friday, 10:00 A.M. to 4:00 P.M., May through October and 10:00 A.M. to 2:00 P.M. the rest of year; closed holidays. Nominal admission fee; (317) 966–2235.

Earlham College, located on the south side of U.S. Highway 40 just west of downtown Richmond, is the home of the **Joseph Moore Museum of Natural Science.** Such wonders as a prehistoric mastadon, an extinct giant beaver, and authentic allosaurus skeletons are displayed, along with Ordovician fossils, arthropods, live snakes, Indiana birds of prey, and a mummy. The museum is open, free of charge, from 1:00 to 4:00 P.M. Monday, Wednesday, and Friday from September through November and January through May; also open 1:00 to 5:00 P.M. Sunday year-round and other times by appointment. A planetarium that is part of the Moore Museum presents free shows at 1:30, 2:30, and 3:30 P.M. each Sunday. Contact Earlham College, West National Road (U.S. Highway 40), Richmond 47374; (317) 983–1303.

◆ **Whitewater Gorge Park,** which borders Whitewater River in the heart of Richmond, is one of only two known places in the United States where a unique type of limestone is exposed to the surface. Geologists, paleontologists, and amateur collectors have been coming to this site for more than a century to examine the abundance of fossils in the gorge's 425-million-year-old rock formations. The park also contains an Audubon bird sanctuary, Thistlethwaite Falls, Middlefork Reservoir, and some scenic fossil collection sites. A 3½-mile-long footpath leads through the gorge,

105

but it's necessary to hike the entire length of it. Trail maps and additional information can be obtained by contacting the Richmond Parks and Recreation Department, Administration Office, 2200 National Road East, Richmond 47374; (317) 983–7274; or the Richmond-Wayne County Convention and Tourism Bureau, 600 Promenade, Richmond 47374; (317) 935–8687 or 1–800–828–8414.

Centerville, about 5 miles west of Richmond on U.S. Highway 40, claims to have the greatest concentration of antiques shops in the United States. ◆ **Webb's Antique Mall** alone covers approximately two acres and boasts some 300 dealers. Contact the mall's office at 200 West Union Street in Centerville; (317) 855–5542 or 855–5551.

Fountain City is the home of the ◆ **Levi Coffin House,** known as "the Grand Central Station of the Underground Railroad." Levi and Catharine Coffin, Quakers who were opposed to slavery, opened their 1839 Federal-style home to approximately 2,000 fugitive black slaves during the Civil War era. You may know the Coffins better as Simeon and Rachel Halliday, characters in *Uncle Tom's Cabin*. Eliza Harris, the heroine of the same book, was a refugee who stayed with the Coffins for several days. The house, located on U.S. Highway 27 North, is open to the public from 1:00 to 4:00 P.M. Tuesday through Sunday, June through mid-September, 1:00 to 4:00 P.M. Saturday and Sunday only the rest of September through October; closed July 4; nominal admission fee. Contact the Levi Coffin House, P.O. Box 77, Fountain City 47341; (317) 847–2432.

Since Guy Welliver bought his Hagerstown restaurant in the 1940s, he has increased its seating capacity from about 50 to 500—and still customers stand in line. They do so patiently, secure in the knowledge that what awaits them at **Welliver's Smorgasbord** is well worth it. Regular patrons include the 2,000 or so lucky people who live in Hagerstown and don't have far to go, as well as diners from all over central Indiana and neighboring Ohio. What lures them is the specialty of the house: an elaborate but reasonably priced buffet that features steamed shrimp in all-you-can-eat quantities. The homemade bread and salad bar are also highly recommended. Welliver's Smorgasbord, located at 40 East Main Street, is open 5:00 to 8:00 P.M. Thursday, 5:00 to 9:00 P.M. Friday, 4:30 to 9:00 P.M. Saturday, and 11:00 A.M. to 8:00 P.M. Sunday (no shrimp on Sunday); (317) 489–4131.

Not far down the road from Welliver's you can spend the night at one of the most luxurious bed-and-breakfast facilities in the Midwest. The ◆ **Teetor House,** a sprawling mansion built as a private home in the 1930s, is surrounded by ten acres of lawns and mature trees. Inside, you can admire the grand player piano, a staircase that duplicates those in New York City's Waldorf Astoria Hotel, a bathroom equipped with an ice-water spigot and a king-size shower with nine shower heads, stained-glass windows, rich tapestries, and polished woods. The entire estate reflects the affluence and taste of its original owner, a self-made millionaire named Ralph Teetor who invented the speedostat (we call it cruise control today). For $75 to $90 a night per couple, guests can stay in one of four bedrooms and enjoy a breakfast served on Lenox china. Contact the Teetor House, 300 West Main Street, Hagerstown 47346; (317) 489–4422.

A short distance away, at 498 South Washington Street, some thirty employees of ◆ **Tedco, Inc.,** make about 30,000 gyroscopes a month for worldwide distribution. One of the toy factory's biggest customers is the Smithsonian Institution. Other popular toys are also produced here. Parents will be pleased to learn that all Tedco toys retail for $2.50 to $10.00. Call (317) 489–4527 to arrange a free tour.

Abbott's Candy Shop, the oldest continuous business in town, uses old family recipes to turn out a cornucopia of confections that are sold at a store in Hagerstown and by mail throughout the country. Its specialty and most popular sweet is the caramel, but many other varieties await visitors, too. Located at 48 East Walnut Street; open 9:00 A.M. to 5:00 P.M. Monday through Friday; also open 9:00 A.M. to 5:00 P.M. Saturday from Thanksgiving to Christmas Eve. Call (317) 489–4442 to arrange a free tour (yes, free samples *are* included).

Brian Bex has spent more than thirty years amassing the largest known collection of ◆ **eagles in art.** Some of his unusual pieces are exhibited at the Indianapolis Museum of Art (see listing under Marion County in the Central Indiana section), but many are displayed at Mr. Bex's complex of business offices in Hagerstown. The eagles appear in a variety of forms, such as paintings and sculptures, and are made from a wide range of materials, including gold, ivory, crystal, porcelain, wood, and copper. Mr. Bex's company, American Communications Network, is located

107

just northeast of Hagerstown at 100 North Woodpecker Road; open 8:30 A.M. to 4:30 P.M. Monday through Friday. Free guided tours, which last approximately one hour, are available by appointment; (317) 489–5566.

SOUTHWEST INDIANA

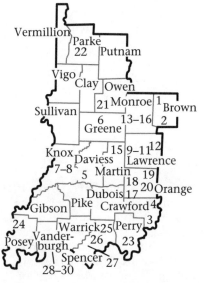

1. John Dillinger Historical Museum
2. Story Inn
3. Wyandotte Cave
4. Marengo Cave
5. Gasthoff Amish Village
6. Greene County viaduct
7. Grouseland
8. Brute Library
9. Limestone quarries
10. Green Hill Cemetery
11. Bluespring Caverns
12. Spring Mill State Park
13. Jangchub Chorten
14. Lilly Library of Rare Books and Manuscripts.
15. Hoagy Carmichael Room
16. indiana University Cyclotron Facility

17. Indiana Railway Museum
18. West Baden Hotel
19. Punkin Center General Store
20. Pioneer Mothers Memorial Forest
21. Barn House
22. Billie Creek Village
23. Tell City Pretzel Company
24. New Harmony
25. St. Meinrad Archabbey
26. Santa Clais
27. Lincoln Boyhood National Memorial
28. John Augustus Reitz Home
29. Wesselman Woods State Nature Preserve
30. Angel Mounds Historic Site

Southwest Indiana
Brown County

Things don't change much in Brown County. The population today is nearly the same as it was in 1880. Each morning the mists rise from hills still draped with forests. Log cabins, hemmed in by split-rail fences, nestle in isolated hollows. Like as not there's a woodpile in the yard, and on cool days fingers of wood smoke spiral up from stone chimneys. Narrow, twisting country roads lead to picturesque places with picturesque names—Gnaw Bone, Bean Blossom, Scarce O'Fat Ridge, Bear Wallow Hill, Milk-Sick Bottoms, Slippery Elm Chute Road, and Booger Holler. No billboards mar your view along the way—they're not allowed in Brown County. No air pollution muddies the landscape and offends your nostrils—Brown County has no industry. And if you're in a hurry, you're out of luck—Brown County doesn't cater to people in a hurry.

Nashville, the county seat and largest town in the county, normally has a population of about 700 people, but on October weekends that figure swells to more than 100,000. Brown County is best known for its dazzling fall color. Most folks head for Brown County State Park, some 15,000 acres of natural beauty near Nashville, but **Yellowood State Forest** in western Brown County and a portion of the southern part of the county offer equally spectacular and less-crowded panoramas.

In spring Brown County is glorious with the blossoms of redbud and dogwood trees and myriad wildflowers. In summer the woods offer a cool green retreat, and for wintertime visitors there are cross-country ski trails and a downhill ski resort.

Brown County first gained fame as a mecca for artists and craftspeople, who have been inspired by the peace and beauty of these hills since the 1870s. Today many open their studios to the public. The **Brown County Art Guild** and the **Brown County Art Gallery,** both in Nashville, are among the galleries that exhibit some of their works.

Nashville is the hub of activity in Brown County—a potpourri of some 250 shops, museums, and restaurants. Craftspeople make and sell quilts, pottery, wood carvings, metal sculptures, hand-carved candles, leather goods, silver and gold jewelry made to order, stained-glass wares, dollhouses, teddy bears, hand-blown art glass, dulcimers, and much more. At many shops you can watch the artisans at work.

Much of Indiana is John Dillinger territory—he was born in Moorseville, and it's believed that he buried much of his still-unrecovered loot from bank robberies in various parts of the Hoosier State. Local old-timers like to relate how James Jenkins, a member of Dillinger's gang, was gunned down in Bean Blossom, just north of Nashville, after a jailbreak. The ◆ **John Dillinger Historical Museum,** located at 90 West Washington Street in Nashville, houses about 95 percent of all known publicly displayed memorabilia of one of this country's most infamous criminals. Among the exhibits are the original tombstone from Dillinger's Indianapolis grave (see Marion County in the Central Indiana section), bank robbery plans written in Dillinger's own hand, the carved wooden pistol he used to escape from a northern Indiana jail, and a vintage Ford Motor Company ad that asks, "Will they catch Dillinger? Not until they get him out of a Ford V-8!" A re-creation of the funeral parlor in which the notorious gangster was laid out, contains a wax likeness of Dillinger in a coffin. Open daily, 10:00 A.M. to 6:00 P.M. March through November, 1:00 to 5:00 P.M. the rest of the year when weather permits. Admission fee; (812) 988–1933.

With no seat more than ten rows from the stage, the **Brown County Playhouse** in the heart of Nashville doesn't have a bad seat in the house. This is Indiana's oldest professional stock theater; performers are from the Theatre and Drama Department at Indiana University in nearby Bloomington (see Monroe County). Kevin Kline, winner of two Tonys and an Academy Award; Patricia Kalember of television's "Sisters"; Jonathan Banks of television's "Wiseguy"; and Howard Ashman, who became an Academy Award-winning lyricist for the Disney films *Aladdin, Beauty and the Beast,* and *The Little Mermaid,* are just a few of the actors who have honed their skills on this stage before going on to bigger things. Showtime is at 8:00 P.M., with nights of performance varying from Wednesday through Sunday during summer and fall months. For an exact schedule and other information, contact the Indiana University Auditorium, Bloomington 47405; (812) 855–1103. In season you can also write the Brown County Play-

111

house, P.O. Box 1187, Nashville 47448; or call (812) 988–2123 from 10:00 A.M. to 5:00 P.M. daily and from 10:00 A.M. to 8:30 P.M. on days of performance.

A complex of authentic nineteenth-century buildings just northeast of the courthouse in Nashville is known collectively as the **Country Museum.** Carding, spinning, and weaving are demonstrated in an old log barn. You'll also see a country doctor's office, a blacksmith's shop, and a log cabin home, all complete with furnishings, and an unusual log jail that claims the distinction of being the only jail in the state that ever permitted a prisoner to be his own keeper: While serving a sentence for bootlegging, the prisoner went wherever he wanted to during the day, locked himself up at night, acted as a guide for tourists, and once aided the sheriff in making an arrest. Open 1:00 to 5:00 P.M. Saturdays, Sundays, and holidays, May through October. Admission fee. The buildings can always be viewed, however, from the outside.

To bluegrass music fans, Bill Monroe is a legend and Bean Blossom is a bluegrass mecca. Monroe has been holding one or more festivals annually on his sprawling Bean Blossom property since the mid-1960s, making this the locale of the longest-running bluegrass festival in the country. The thousands of devotees who come here from all over the country and beyond say the Bean Blossom bluegrass festivals have an ambience unlike any other in the world. When professional musicians aren't playing on stage, amateur musicians in the audience are playing in their own impromptu groups. It's a rare moment when there's no music to be heard anywhere.

Most people stay on the festival grounds for the three or four days a festival is held. A campground on the property offers both modern and primitive campsites. In 1992 Monroe brought his extensive collection of bluegrass and country music memorabilia to Bean Blossom and opened his **Bluegrass Hall of Fame and Museum.** Recognized as the father of bluegrass, Monroe accumulated his collection throughout sixty some years of entertaining.

One of the fourteen rooms in the 5,000-square-foot museum is filled with Bill Monroe's personal mementos. Country music artifacts include items once owned by Johnny Cash, Dolly Parton, and Dottie West. On the grounds near the museum is a log cabin that was moved here log by log from Nashville, Tennessee. Known as Uncle Pen's Cabin, it belonged to a relative who took young Bill Monroe into his home when Monroe's parents died. Fans will recognize the name from a song Monroe wrote about his uncle. (It was recorded by Ricky Skaggs and Porter Wagoner.)

The museum, campground, and festival park are located on the east side of State Road 135 in Bean Blossom, about 5 miles north of Nashville. Open daily spring through fall; hours may vary. For additional information call (812) 988–6422 or 988–0333 in season. The rest of the year, call Bill Monroe's winter headquarters in Nashville, Tennessee—(615) 868-3333. The Brown County Convention and Visitors Bureau (see address and phone number at the end of this section) also can provide you with up-to-date information.

Fans of another type of music head to the Red Barn Theatre, about a mile east of Nashville on the south side of State Road 46. Some folks may think Elvis hangs out in a laundromat in Minnesota, as has often been reported, but you'll never convince the folks hereabouts. They'll tell you that Elvis lives in southern Indiana.

The Elvis they're talking about is, of course, an Elvis impersonator, but Bruce Borders is an Elvis impersonator extraordinaire. Bruce has appeared (in one of his Elvis jumpsuits) on several national television shows, including the *CBS News,* the *Late Show with David Letterman,* and the *Oprah* show, and he numbers actress Melanie Griffith among his fans. He's also been asked to appear in a movie and to audition for a Broadway show, but Bruce prefers to do most of his entertaining close to home so he can keep his day job. Bruce, you see, is the mayor of Jasonville, Indiana—a job he's held since 1987.

Although the kudos he's earned impersonating Elvis have received more publicity, Bruce is no slouch as a mayor, either. He took a town that had been operating in the red for many years and put it in the black.

Because he is believed to be the only combination mayor/Elvis impersonator in North America, Bruce owns the copyright for the name **The Mayor of Rock-n-Roll.** You can see The Mayor perform at the Red Barn Theatre at 8:00 P.M. Friday and at 6:30 and 9:30 P.M. Saturday, March through December. Prices are reasonable, and a discount is given for tickets purchased before the day of the show. Tickets are available at the Remember When restaurant adjacent to the theater or at the theater door, beginning at

1:00 P.M., on performance dates. For additional information contact The Mayor of Rock-n-Roll, P.O. Box 1729, Nashville 47448; (812) 988–2679.

For information about any and all of Brown County's attractions, contact the Brown County Convention and Visitors Bureau, Van Buren and Main streets, P.O. Box 840, Nashville 47448; (812) 988–7303 or 1–800–753–3255.

A little farther east of Nashville on State Road 46 is the northern entrance to **Brown County State Park,** accessible via Indiana's only divided, two-lane covered bridge (circa 1838). Enjoy 27 miles of scenic roads, hiking and bridle trails, a nature center, campgrounds (including one for horseback riders), an archery range, an Olympic-size swimming pool, a lodge with a restaurant, and rustic rental cabins. A nature trail leads through **Ogle Hollow State Nature Preserve,** noteworthy for its rare yellowwood trees. Open year-round during daylight hours; vehicle entrance fee April through October. Contact Brown County State Park, P.O. Box 608, Nashville 47448; (812) 988–6406. For lodge and cabin reservations contact Abe Martin Lodge, P.O. Box 547, Nashville 47448; (812) 988–4418.

Continuing east from the park on State Road 46, you'll come to State Road 135, which leads south into a secluded and little-known part of Brown County. Follow State Road 135 to an area referred to locally as **Stone Head,** so called because of the unique monument by the side of the highway that serves as a road sign— a white stone head atop a stone pillar. Every once in a while a prankster makes off with the carving, but an outraged community has always managed to recover it.

Proceed on State Road 135 to the tiny community of Story. Virtually unchanged since its founding in the 1850s, the peaceful hamlet exudes the charm of a Brown County that was—a long-ago Brown County whose rural serenity and beauty first lured artists and craftspeople to these forested hills. Here, amid a cluster of tumbledown buildings that bear mute testimony to old dreams, the ✦ **Story Inn** offers food and shelter so pleasing that the Indiana Division of Tourism has bestowed its "best bed-and-breakfast in the state" award on it. On the outside, the tin-faced, tin-roofed building resembles the general store it once was. On the inside, antiques and knickknacks line the walls of the dining room, and a potbellied stove stands ready to serve on cold winter days. The food, however, is pure gourmet. Such offerings as rabbit New Orleans, chicken Provençal, and Greek spinach pie appear on a menu that changes weekly but always features fresh fish and a pasta dish. No matter what entrée you decide on, save room for dessert—the turtle cheesecake, with its chocolate graham cracker crust and thick caramel topping, is to die for. Guests who spend the night can stay in one of the inn's five upstairs bedrooms or in one of the renovated village cottages nearby; a full country breakfast is included in the inn's room rates of $71 to $82 or the cottages' rates of $82 to $104 per night for two. All rooms have private baths and air-conditioning but no television or telephone. The inn serves three meals a day; prices are moderate to expensive. Advance reservations are recommended for dinner and are required for overnight accommodations. Contact the Story Inn at 6404 South State Road 135, Nashville 47448; or call (812) 988–2273.

Back on State Road 46, about 4 miles east of Nashville, is the hamlet of Gnaw Bone. In late summer and autumn you can find your way here by following the tantalizing aromas. That's when the area's sugarcane is pressed down into sap at a horse-driven mill, then boiled down to molasses at the **Brown County Sorghum Mill.** You can purchase the sorghum, persimmon pudding, cob honey, sorghum cakes, persimmon and black walnut fudge, apple butter, and cider—the latter by the gallon or glass. Hours may vary but are usually 8:00 A.M. to sunset daily, September through November.

At Helmsburg, situated along State Road 45 in northwest Brown County, a small factory near the railroad tracks houses the **Cullum Broom & Mop Co.** The decor and machinery belong to an early-twentieth-century era. Owner James Cullum makes sturdy corn brooms and sassafras fireplace sweepers before your eyes. They're sold in stores throughout the Midwest, but you can also buy them on the spot. Visitors are welcome 8:00 A.M. to 3:00 P.M. Monday through Friday. Contact Cullum Broom & Mop Co., Helmsburg 47435; (812) 988–4897.

Brown County's hills are just that—hills. The highest point in the county is 1,489 feet above sea level, but there's still a respectable downhill ski and snow boarding area on State Road 46 southwest of Nashville that offers all the makings for a fine winter holiday—eight slopes and trails with a vertical drop of 250 feet, a bunny slope for beginners, chair lifts, rope tows, a lodge, a ski shop, and dining facilities. **Ski World** also hosts the annual Brown County Winter Fest, held in early February. Activities during the rest of the year include an Alpine Slide, one of only a handful in the United States (riders slide down one of two twisting concrete tracks in carts). Visitors will also find two 60-foot-high water slides, go-cart and bumper boat rides, bank shot basketball, batting cages, and, during spring through fall weekends, live entertainment. Open 10:00 A.M. to 10:00 P.M. Monday through Thursday, 10:00 A.M. to 4:00 A.M. Friday, 9:00 A.M. to 4:00 A.M. Saturday, and 9:00 A.M. to 10:00 P.M. Sunday during ski season; noon to 8:00 P.M. weekends and holidays in the spring and fall; 11:00 A.M. to 10:00 P.M. daily in the summer (weather permitting); closed Christmas Eve. Contact Ski World, P.O. Box 445, Nashville 47448; (812) 988–6638.

Tourists, as well as armies, travel on their stomachs. The most popular of the many fine eateries in Nashville is the **Nashville House,** located on the corner of Main and Van Buren streets in the center of town. Its charming, rustic atmosphere is enhanced by antique furniture, checkered tablecloths, and a huge stone fireplace. The menu lists such Hoosier favorites as fried ham steak, baked ham, barbecue ribs, roast turkey, country fried chicken, and hot or iced sassafras tea, but the highlight of any meal has to be the fried biscuits. These delicious deep-fried dough balls, served with baked apple butter, could make an addict of anyone. Owner Andy Rogers says they were invented by his father, Jack Rogers, around 1947. The Nashville House is no place for dieters—not only is everything sinfully fattening, but unless you're a lumberjack you might be hard put to eat everything that's placed in front of you. Although the menu is limited, the food is country cooking at its finest. Prices range from $3.50 to $9.50 for lunch and from $12 to $20 for dinner; children's menu. Open 11:30 A.M. to 8:00 P.M. Sunday through Thursday and 11:30 A.M. to 9:00 P.M. Friday and Saturday in October; closed Tuesday the rest of the year; also closed for two weeks during the Christmas season. Reservations are accepted except during October; (812) 988–4554.

The entrance to the Nashville House is through the **Old Country Store,** a pleasant place to browse if you have to wait for seating in the restaurant. It's just what the name implies—a delightful clutter of goods that includes many hard-to-find items from yesteryear.

Need a cup of hot brew and a pleasant corner in which to relax a spell? Drop in at **The Daily Grind.** You'll find it in Nashville's

Calvin Place, a cluster of shops on the southwest corner of Franklin and Van Buren streets. Although coffeehouses have dropped from the scene in many places, this one is alive and well, thank you. No one gets sticky about it, but from the moment you lift the latch and walk through the heavy wooden door you feel welcome here. Your main problem will be making a decision. There are nearly twenty different gourmet coffees from all over the world and fifty varieties of tea—all served in stoneware mugs. Go-withs include salads, sandwiches, soup, bagels, and pastries. Belgian waffles, sausages, and croissants filled with ham, eggs, and cheese are popular breakfast fare. Stored on the mantel of the stone fireplace is a selection of such games as chess, checkers, and backgammon—help yourself. Read one of the newspapers lying about or play a game of darts. The country store area offers coffee beans, apothecary jars filled with tea leaves, coffee mugs, spices, teapots, and coffeemakers. The Daily Grind, which fills mail orders, is open year-round 8:00 A.M. to 6:00 P.M. Sunday through Thursday, and 8:00 A.M. to 10:00 P.M. Friday and Saturday. Live entertainment is featured on Friday and Saturday nights at 7:00 P.M.. Hours may vary in the winter. Contact The Daily Grind, P.O. Box 607, Nashville 47448; (812) 988–4808.

Overnight facilities in and near Nashville range from resort inns to motels, from bed-and-breakfast rooms in private homes to furnished log cabins with equipped kitchens. Many are booked up as much as two years in advance, especially on weekends from spring through fall and the week before Christmas, so plan ahead. For more information contact the Brown County Convention & Visitors Bureau, P.O. Box 840, Nashville 47448; (812) 988–7303 or 1–800–753–3255.

While in Nashville buy a copy of the *Brown County Democrat,* which has been honored as Indiana's finest weekly newspaper more times than anyone can remember. The "Sheriff's Log" therein is a Brown County classic. You'll find such entries as:

Man called and said he just put on a pot of coffee if any officers are in the area and want coffee.

Girl at restaurant requests a conservation officer. An owl is sitting on the pizza oven.

Trouble reported at the city dump. Someone abandoned a person there.

A coon is asleep on the shelf [of a local shop] with a teddy bear.

117

Man wants deputy [any deputy] to meet him so that he can bor-
    row $5 or $10.
Man requests Nashville town marshal go to restaurant and check
    the stove to see if he left a pot of beans on.
Caller says someone has been cow tipping. His cows were asleep
    in the field and someone tipped them over.

Like the mythical sheriff's office in Mayberry, North Carolina, made famous by a television series, this one's run with a lot of heart.

CRAWFORD COUNTY

Most spelunkers are aware of the subterranean wonders that exist in the Hoosier State, but few other people know that there is a proliferation of caves in southern Indiana. Several of those open to the public are in Crawford County.

Thanks to being mentioned in both *Ripley's Believe It or Not* and the *Guinness Book of World Records*, ❖ **Wyandotte Cave** has become world-famous for its Monument Mountain—the highest underground mountain in any known cave on earth. It stands 135 feet tall, the focal point of an awe-inspiring room known as Rothrock's Cathedral, which is approximately 185 feet high, 360 feet long, and 140 feet wide. Your tour guide may introduce you to the ghost of Chief Wyandotte, a weird and entertaining play of shadows at the top of the cathedral. Superlatives apply elsewhere in the cave, too: a room a half-mile in circumference and 200 feet high is the largest subterranean room known anywhere in the world, and a resplendent stalagmite 35 feet high and 75 feet around is believed to be the world's largest formation of its kind. With some 25 miles of known passages explored, the cave itself is among the earth's largest. You'll also see delicate and exquisite formations called helictites that are extremely rare. A two-hour walk covers 1½ miles; if you're the rugged type, opt for a five- or eight-hour tour during which you'll not only walk but crawl, climb, descend a pole once used by Indians, and, in places, travel by lantern light.

Just south of Wyandotte Cave is **Little Wyandotte Cave,** which can be toured in about thirty minutes. This cave is much more ordinary but is enjoyable for those who've never been in a cavern.

To reach the caves travel west from Corydon on State Road 62 for about 12 miles and turn north on a blacktop road; signs point the way. Admission fees; reservations necessary for the five- and eight-hour tours. Although available all year, tours are conducted more frequently in the summer. Nature provides a constant temperature of fifty-two degrees all year long for both caves. Caves and vistior center open daily Memorial Day through Labor Day; closed Monday the rest of the year. Contact Wyandotte Caves, Route 1, Box 85, Leavenworth 47137; (812) 738–2782.

The state-owned caves are part of a larger recreation area known as the **Harrison-Crawford Wyandotte Complex.** Besides the caves it includes the **Wyandotte Woods State Recreation Area** and the **Harrison-Crawford State Forest,** both of which straddle the Harrison-Crawford county line. Wyandotte Woods offers developed campsites, hiking and bridle trails, a nature center, views of the Ohio River, and an Olympic-size swimming pool. For those who enjoy roughing it, Harrison-Crawford State Forest has primitive campsites and overnight backpacking trails. To reach both, travel west from Corydon on State Road 62 for about 8 miles to State Road 462 and turn south; State Road 462 runs through the forest and ends in Wyandotte Woods. For information about both the forest and the recreation area, contact Harrison-Crawford State Forest, 7240 Old Forest Road, Corydon 47112; (812) 738–8232.

Not far north of Wyandotte Caves is ◆ **Marengo Cave,** discovered in 1883 by a young brother and sister exploring a sinkhole. The cave, a comfortable fifty-four degrees at all times, has been open to the public ever since, and its beauty has been acclaimed throughout the world. Concerts were once held in a subterranean room noted for its acoustics, and an early-day evangelist preached his fiery message from Pulpit Rock. Underground weddings and dances were regular occurrences throughout the years, and a square dance is still held in the Music Hall Chamber each July.

Two tours are offered. The highlight of the ½-mile tour is Crystal Palace, acknowledged by speleologists as one of the ten most beautiful cavern rooms anywhere. A 1-mile tour through a different part of the cave features totem pole stalagmites and a cavern possibly big enough to build a highway through. Above the cavern is a 112-acre park, complete with campsites and trail rides atop horses from the park's stables. Separate fee for each tour; special combination price for both. Cave open daily year-round, except Thanksgiving and Christmas; 9:00 A.M. to 6:00 P.M. Memorial Day to Labor Day and spring and fall weekends; 9:30 A.M. to 5:30 P.M. spring and fall weekdays; 9:00 A.M. to 5:00 P.M. the rest of the year. Marengo Cave is just northeast of the town of Marengo; go east from Marengo on State Road 64/66 and follow the signs. Contact Marengo Cave Park, Marengo Cave Road, P.O. Box 217, Marengo 47140; (812) 365–2705.

Twisting its way southward through Crawford County is the lovely, spring-fed **Blue River,** Indiana's first officially designated natural and scenic river and an ideal canoe stream. Several outfitters offer trips, ranging from 7 to 58 miles in length; on longer trips you spend the night on the river. Depending on the trip you take, you'll float quiet waters and shoot rapids; pass caves, springs, limestone bluffs, and walls of trees; or make your way around rock gardens and through narrow gorges. The fishing is some of the best in the Midwest, producing catches of bass, crappie, bluegill, and catfish, and the serenity can be well-nigh incredible. In its lower stretches, just before it joins the Ohio River, the Blue River turns sluggish—perfect for tubing. Rates for canoeing range from $7.50 to $21.00 per person and include paddle, life jacket, and shuttle service; special rates for children. The season is usually April through October, but water levels are best for canoeing before mid-July. For names of outfitters in the area, contact the Crawford County Chamber of Commerce, Route 1, Box 224D, Marengo 47140, (812) 365–2174 or 1–800–742–6763.

Just west of Milltown, on the north side of State Road 64, is an **old limestone quarry** with an intriguing maze of tunnels dug into the side of a hill. Inside the cavernous excavations, eerie echoes bombard your ears—the flutter of birds' wings, dripping water, your own footsteps. Ceilings at least 20 feet high, supported by great stone buttresses, and the silent halls they enclose create the impression that you are entering some ancient catacombs or perhaps a cathedral, now hushed and still, whose days of glory have been lost in the mists of time. Explore at your own risk.

The little town of Leavenworth on the Ohio River likens its history to that of Noah and the ark—the oldest establishments in town date back to just after the flood. The granddaddy of all floods on the Ohio occurred in 1937, and most of the riverside town of Leavenworth was washed away to points south.

Undaunted, residents moved up to a blufftop and started over. Lack of money, like politics, can make for strange bedfellows, so a small cafe and a grocery store shared the second floor of a chicken hatchery. From those humble beginnings has evolved a family restaurant called **The Overlook,** which now occupies the entire building. Through the years the restaurant has specialized in good home cooking and reasonable prices, and people go out of their way to stop here. Even if the food weren't so good it would be worth stopping at The Overlook just for a view—a sweeping panorama of forested hills and the broad Ohio River as it arches around a horseshoe bend. Outside stands what is believed to be the largest redbud tree in the world. The Overlook, located on the south side of State Road 62 in Leavenworth, is open 8:00 A.M. to 9:00 P.M. daily year-round, except Christmas, for breakfast, lunch, and dinner. Dinner prices range from $7.00 to $16.00. Contact The Overlook, P.O. Box 67, Leavenworth 47137; (812) 739–4264.

DAVIESS COUNTY

Along about 1972 the local folks decided they needed a unique attraction to put Daviess County on the map, and their idea brought them fame that exceeded their wildest expectations. They combined Indiana's best-known event, the Indianapolis 500, with Daviess County's best-known product—turkeys—and gave birth to the **Turkey Trot Festival.**

Come September, turkeydom's finest make their way to Montgomery Recreation Park in Montgomery for four days of the most laughable racing imaginable. Because there are about forty turkeys to every human being in Daviess County (with a noticeable but temporary change in the ratio just after the Thanksgiving and Christmas holidays), there can be a lot of birds to face off. This requires many preliminary heats, and only the cream of the crop survive the grueling schedule to race in the final championship run.

On the last, fateful day, anxious jockeys lead their tethered birds to the starting line, eager to put weeks of training to the test. Some raw talent is always on hand, too, since many owners believe that training a bird with a brain the size of a man's thumbnail is a waste of time. Onlookers cheer their personal favorites—

such racing greats as Dirty Bird, White Lightning, and Turkey Lurkey.

On signal, the turkeys head down a 213-foot-long straightaway track toward a finish line that, for a top turkey trotter, is approximately twenty seconds away. Alas, prima donnas are inevitable. Some refuse to start at all. The more befuddled go sideways or backward. Still others tire along the way and pause to peck at whatever turkeys like to peck at. Some even take to the air, disdainfully rising above it all. Eventually, however, one galloping gobbler manages to cross the finish line and is declared the grand champion.

Another big event is the best-dressed turkey contest, which inspires elaborate costumes. One recent winner devastated the judges when she modeled her stunning powder-blue bikini, then further charmed them by coyly batting her false eyelashes.

And if you think they don't take all this seriously in Daviess County, consider the fact that these are the only turkey races in the world sanctioned by the National Turkey Federation. The races have received national attention from the day of their inception, and stories about them have been translated into five foreign languages and printed all around the globe. Spectators come from all over.

Although the turkeys are obviously the main attraction, the festival also features mud volleyball, a demolition derby, tractor pulls, and entertainment by top country music stars. For additional information contact the Daviess County Visitors Bureau, 1 Train Depot Street, P.O. Box 430, Washington 47501; (812) 254–5262.

Montgomery is located in the heart of southern Indiana's Amish country, a fact that until recently was little known beyond the borders of Daviess County and its immediate neighbors. To celebrate this heritage, the sixty-five-acre ◆ **Gasthoff Amish Village** is being constructed on the Henry Wittmer farm near Montgomery. At this writing, visitors will find a restaurant that features authentic Amish cooking, a gift shop that sells items handmade by Amish craftspeople, an outdoor flea market (Tuesday and Wednesday, May through October), and a year-round farmer's market. Future plans include the addition of an inn, an auction barn, and shops that will house various Amish businesses. Located just north of Montgomery on County Road 650E, the village is open 8:00 A.M. to 8:00 P.M. Monday through Thursday and 8:00 A.M. to 9:00 P.M. Friday and Saturday during summer months; 11:00 A.M. to 8:00 P.M. Monday through Thursday, 11:00 A.M. to 9:00 P.M. Friday, and 8:00 A.M. to 9:00 P.M. Saturday the rest of the year. Call (812) 486–3977.

Guided tours of the surrounding area are available for groups of fifteen or more; visitors are taken to Amish communities and to such Amish businesses as a quilt shop, a buggy factory, a candy factory, and a country store. Tours, which include a meal at the village's restaurant, are offered at 9:00 A.M. and 1:00 P.M. Monday through Saturday year-round; reservations must be made at least ten days in advance. For tour reservations and updated information about the village, contact the Daviess County Development Company, Inc., P.O. Box 7, Montgomery 47558; (812) 486–3354.

GREENE COUNTY

No matter what you've read or been told, there is no way to fully prepare you for your first glimpse of the ◈ **Greene County viaduct.** One minute you're driving along an isolated rural road that winds through wooded hills and hollows; the next minute you're suddenly confronted with an open valley and the massive railroad trestle that spans it—one of the most spectacular sights in the state.

Completed in 1906 as part of the Illinois Central Railroad line, the viaduct is 180 feet high and 2,295 feet long—the second longest in the world. (To see the longest, you'll have to travel to Cantal, France.) Park beneath the massive steel girders that support it, and climb a well-worn path up the hill at the north end for a sweeping view.

The viaduct is located just south of a road that links Solsberry and the hamlet of Tulip. Head west from Solsberry on the country road that parallels the railroad tracks. After driving about 5 miles, you'll come to County Road 480E, which turns off to the south and leads beneath the trestle.

It's best to stop at the general store in Solsberry and ask for exact directions. Roads are not well marked hereabouts, and besides, it's great fun to listen to the yarns being spun by any occupants of the store's "liar's bench." Maybe they'll tell you the one about the man wearing gum rubber boots who fell off the viaduct while it was being constructed and bounced for three days. He finally had to be shot to keep him from starving to death; for additional information contact the Bloomfield Chamber of Commerce, 6 East Main Street, P.O. Box 144, Bloomfield 47424; (812) 384–8995.

In the vast, dense forest that covered most of Indiana during the last century, there grew a **huge sycamore** that was the largest tree in the eastern half of the United States. Naturalists and historians advised everyone to go to Worthington and see this wonderful tree, which stood 150 feet high, spread its branches to a length of 100 feet, and measured more than 42 feet in circumference at 5 feet above the ground.

In 1920 a storm toppled it, and the town of Worthington decided to preserve one of its limbs in a place of honor. That limb, more than 23 feet in circumference and larger than the trunks of most trees in Indiana today, can be seen in Worthington's City Park at the north end of town. You can't miss it—it's the only tree in the park with a roof over its head.

KNOX COUNTY

Vincennes, Indiana's oldest city, has a colorful history, and the town abounds with monuments to its past. George Rogers Clark came here during the American Revolution to battle the British, and his deeds are memorialized in the twenty-four-acre **George Rogers Clark National Historical Park,** located at 401 South Second Street (open 9:00 A.M. to 5:00 P.M. daily, except major winter holidays). Within a magnificent round stone structure are seven murals depicting Clark's campaigns. Living-history programs, featured on some summer weekends, re-create camp life with military drills and firearm demonstrations. Nominal admission fee for memorial building, visitor center free; (812) 882–1776.

At the **Indiana Territory State Historic Site,** at the corner of First and Harrison streets on the western edge of the Vincennes University campus, is a two-story white frame building that served as the capitol for the Indiana Territory from 1811 to 1813. Nearby is the *Western Sun* Print Shop where the territory's first newspaper was published on July 4, 1804; the wooden printing press seen by today's visitors is the same type as the original. Legend has it that Abe Lincoln, a faithful reader of the *Sun,* came here as a young man to study a printing press in operation and actually helped print the Saturday, March 6, 1830, edition of the paper on the day of his visit. Donations accepted. Open 9:00 A.M. to 5:00 P.M. Wednesday through Saturday, 1:00 to 5:00 P.M. Sunday, mid-March through December. Contact P.O. Box 81, Vincennes 47591; (812) 882–7472.

◆ **Grouseland,** an early-nineteenth-century Georgian mansion, was the home of William Henry Harrison when he served as the first governor of the Indiana Territory. (He later became the ninth president of the United States and was the grandfather of the twenty-third.) As part of his official duties, he once invited Indian Chief Tecumseh to his home to discuss their differences. Tecumseh refused to come inside, saying he preferred to sit on the earth, his mother, and so the two men held council in a walnut grove on the front lawn. Located at 3 West Scott Street; (812) 882–2096. Open daily, 9:00 A.M. to 5:00 P.M., March through December, except Thanksgiving and Christmas; 11:00 A.M. to 4:00 P.M. January and February, except New Year's Day; admission fee.

The boundaries of the Indiana Territory first encompassed the present-day states of Indiana, Illinois, Michigan, Wisconsin, and part of Minnesota, and later the lands included in the 1803 Louisiana Purchase. So tiny Vincennes, with Harrison at its helm, was for a while the seat of government for most of the United States from the Alleghenies to the Rockies.

Harrison also served as one of the first trustees of Vincennes University. Founded in 1801, it is the oldest university west of the Alleghenies.

St. Francis Xavier Cathedral, dating back to 1702, is the oldest Catholic church in Indiana. The present redbrick building is actually the fourth church to stand on this site; its first two predecessors were built of logs, while the third, also a brick structure, was built in 1826 and rebuilt later the same year after a storm nearly destroyed it. Rich, dark cedars shelter the serene grounds of the **Old French Cemetery** adjacent to the cathedral, where priests, laymen, Indians, soldiers, and black slaves lie buried, many in unmarked graves. The first interment was in 1741, the last in 1846. Cathedral located at 205 Church Street; open 7:00 A.M. to 4:00 P.M. daily. Call (812) 882–5638 or 886–1141.

Behind the cathedral, housed in a modern redbrick building, is ◆ **Brute Library,** the oldest library in Indiana, containing

Grouseland

more than 11,000 rare books and documents. Bishop Simon Brute (1779–1839), the first Bishop of Vincennes, assembled the collection in France and brought it with him to the wilderness that was the Indiana Territory. He was called by President John Quincy Adams "the most learned man of his day in America."

A papal bull of Pope John XXII, dated 1319 and written on heavy parchment, is the oldest manuscript in the library. The oldest book, dated 1476, glows with the lustrous colors of hand illumination, and the parchment still bears the holes made by the pins that held the pages in place while the illuminating was done. Another interesting volume contains the Lord's Prayer in 250 different languages. In addition there are old maps, letters, and a certified copy of a license issued on March 6, 1833, to Abraham Lincoln and William Berry, permitting them to operate a tavern in New Salem, Illinois. Nominal admission fee; open 11:00 A.M. to 4:00 P.M. daily May through August; (812) 882–5638.

Built about 1806, the **Brouillet French House** at 509 North First Street is one of the few remaining upright log-and-mud houses in North America. Inside are the original fireplace and warming oven, along with authentic period furnishings. Open 1:00 to 5:00 P.M., Tuesday through Sunday; free admission; (812) 882–7886.

A remnant of prehistory, the 140-foot-high **Sonotabac Indian Mound** was constructed about 300 B.C. You can journey even further back in time within the museum at the mound's base, where exhibits and artifacts date back to 8000 B.C. Admission fee. Open daily 10:00 A.M. to 4:00 P.M. (Sunday 1:00 to 4:00 p.m.) May through September and weekends in October. Call (812) 882–7679. Grounds open daily, dawn to dusk; free admission. Located on the south side of Wabash Avenue about ½ mile east of Thirteenth Street; look for signs. Several other Indian mounds lie to the east and south of Vincennes.

Red Skelton, the beloved comedian, was born in Vincennes at 111 West Lyndale Avenue. A sign in front of the house commemorates the occasion. When Red was just ten years old he joined the Hagenbach-Wallace Circus (which wintered in Peru, Indiana) as a clown.

For additional information contact the Vincennes Area Chamber of Commerce, 27 North Third Street, Vincennes 47591; (812) 882–6440 or (800) 886–6443.

LAWRENCE COUNTY

For more than one hundred years, many of the great public edifices in this country have been constructed with Indiana limestone. Architects favor it because it lends itself easily to carving and the most delicate tracery when first quarried, then becomes hard and durable when exposed to atmospheric agents. Just a few of the structures that are built at least partly of oolitic limestone (so called because of its granular composition, which suggests a mass of fish eggs) from the Bedford area are the Empire State Building (it withstood King Kong, you know) and Rockefeller Center in New York City; Washington National Cathedral (eighty-three years in the making, it was completed on September 29, 1990, when a crane placed a 1,000-pound chunk of intricately carved Indiana limestone atop one of the church's towers); the Pentagon; the Lincoln Memorial; Chicago's Merchandise Mart; and the University of Moscow (yes, the one in Russia!).

The ◆ **limestone quarries** are quite impressive to see—great gaping cavities in the earth from which are extracted immense blocks of stone that average 4 feet in thickness, 10 feet in width, and from 50 to 100 feet in length. Before being removed from the quarry floor, they're broken into small blocks for easy transportation to a processing mill. To view the quarries, go north from Bedford on State Road 37 through Oolitic; the quarries are about a half-mile north of Oolitic.

When you pass through Oolitic, stop and meet a new town resident—a limestone **statue of Joe Palooka,** which stands in front of the town hall on Main Street. A famous comic strip character from the not-too-distant past, Joe was at the peak of his popularity in the 1940s. A paragon of good, Joe was an earthbound Superman of sorts who championed democracy and decency and was an inspiration to the youth of his day. He was also a boxer, and he is depicted—10 feet tall and weighing more than ten tons—wearing trunks and boxing gloves.

A few years ago, the Bedford Industrial Development Foundation, a nonprofit financial arm of the Chamber of Commerce, opened a twenty-acre limestone demonstration center that overlooks the two largest quarries. A museum was built, displays of machinery and tools were set up, and construction was begun on the two main attractions—a ⅛-scale limestone reproduction of the

Great Pyramid of Cheops and a 650-foot duplication of a segment from the Great Wall of China. The project was eventually abandoned due to lack of funds, but every once in a while someone decides to have a go at reviving it—thus far to no avail. Known locally as "the pyramid," the park-to-be now consists of a rusting Quonset hut that was meant to serve as the museum, a jumble of limestone boulders, and signs that proclaim this to be the LIMESTONE TOURIST PARK. For current information on the on-again, off-again tourist attraction, which lies on a fifteen-acre lot about 9 miles north of Bedford via State Road 37, contact the Lawrence County Tourism Bureau, 1116 Sixteenth Street, P.O. Box 1193, Bedford 47421; (812) 275–7637 or 1–800–798–0769.

Bedford stone, another name for local limestone, is sometimes used for gravestones, and many fine examples can be seen in ❖ **Green Hill Cemetery,** 1202 Eighteenth Street in Bedford; (812) 275–5110. The monument for Louis Baker, a twenty-three-year-old apprentice stonecutter who died suddenly in 1917, was carved by his grieving fellow workers; they reproduced his workbench, fully detailed even to actual size, exactly as he had left it for the last time. The statue of Michael F. Wallner preserves his doughboy uniform down to the most minute crease. Also seen in the cemetery are some of the tree-trunk carvings that were popular around the turn of the century, including one adorned with high-button shoes and a straw hat that memorializes a seven-year-old girl who died in 1894. These and other of Green Hill's monuments have been featured on several national television shows. Free walking-tour maps of the cemetery are available from the Lawrence County Tourism Bureau (see the preceding paragraph for address and phone numbers).

On the south side of State Road 158, about 3 miles west of Bedford, you can visit **Elliott Special Products, Inc.,** a small limestone milling operation that creates many unique items from local limestone. A combination showroom/gift shop on the premises is open seasonally; call for hours. A rugged, ¼-mile-long, self-guided walking path leads visitors past the stacking yard of a working quarry and an abandoned quarry; the path is accessible when the showroom is open. Contact Elliott Special Products, Inc., P.O. Box 1267, Bedford 47421; (812) 275–1900, for additional information.

At Purdue University's **Feldun Purdue Agricultural Center,** you can roam the 449 acres of the Moses Fell Farm. Mr. Fell donated the farm to Purdue University in 1914, and it has been used ever since for experimental purposes. Located on State Road 458, which runs north off State Road 158, 3 miles west of Bedford; signs point the way. Open daily year-round, 6:30 A.M. to 5:30 P.M. Monday through Saturday and 6:30 A.M. to 4:00 P.M. Sunday; free admission. Contact Feldun Purdue Agricultural Center, Dark Hollow Road, Bedford 47421; (812) 275–6327.

Southwest of Bedford our country's longest "lost river" flows through a startling subterranean world. More than 20 miles of passageways have currently been explored at ◆ **Bluespring Caverns,** one of the world's ten longest, and most of those miles are wet ones—inundated by a system of underground streams. Visitors descend a stairway into a sinkhole entrance room, then venture 4,000 feet into the yawning depths aboard flat-bottomed boats that glide silently through a world of total darkness. The rare white fish and crayfish that live in these waters are blind, having adapted themselves over the years to a habitat where sight is of no use. Lights mounted on the bottom of the tour boat create shifting shadows on fluted walls and provide unique glimpses of water-sculpted formations on the mirrorlike surface of the stream. By prior arrangement you can also participate in a "wild tour," which includes exploration of some of the dry portions of the cave, crawling, climbing, and an underground slide show.

This is one place where weather will never surprise you—the temperature is a constant fifty-two degrees year-round. To reach Bluespring Caverns Park from Bedford, go south on U.S. Highway 50 for about 6 miles, then turn west on County Road 4505 for about a half-mile; signs point the way. Open 9:00 A.M. to 6:00 P.M. daily, May through September; Saturday and Sunday, April and October. Last tour leaves at 5:00 P.M. Admission fee. Campsites with water and electricity are available in the park. Contact Bluespring Caverns Park, RR 11, Box 988, Bedford 47421; (812) 279–9471.

The many attractions at ◆ **Spring Mill State Park** span a time period from the early 1800s to the threshold of the space age. As a boy growing up in nearby Mitchell, Virgil I. (Gus) Grissom loved this park. Grissom grew up to become one of the seven original astronauts and, in 1965, the second American in space. Two years later he was dead—one of three astronauts killed in a tragic spacecraft fire at Cape Kennedy. The *Gemini III* capsule in which he made his historic flight now rests, along with his spacesuit and other items related to space travel, in **Grissom Memorial Visitor Center** (P.O. Box 376, Mitchell 47446; 812–849–4129). Open daily year-round.

Nestled in a small valley among the park's wooded hills is a pioneer village that was founded in 1814. Its sawmill, meetinghouse, apothecary, hatmaker's and weaver's shops, water-powered gristmill, general store, tavern, distillery, post office, and log cabin homes have all been restored, and from April through October they are alive with inhabitants who go about their daily routine just as their long-ago counterparts did. You can purchase cornmeal ground at the old gristmill and products from the weaver's looms, and, on occasion, you can participate in candlelight tours of the tiny settlement.

Plants in the **Hamer Pioneer Gardens** are the same as those grown by the village's original occupants; some were used for medicine, some for cooking, and some simply to add beauty to a life that was often harsh. Uphill from the village is a pioneer cemetery that dates back to 1832. The stone markers provide a genealogical history of the town below.

During the spring and summer, nearly every variety of wildflower and bird indigenous to Indiana is found here, and to protect some of the 1,300-acre park's finest natural features the state has set aside two areas as nature preserves. A 2½-mile-loop hiking trail, the most beautiful in the park, winds through **Donaldson's Woods State Nature Preserve,** an outstanding 76-acre virgin forest dominated by giant tulip trees and white oaks. Six acres surrounding the mouth of **Donaldson Cave,** reached by another trail, have also been designated a state nature preserve. The scene that meets your eye here—a small stream flowing from the cave's entrance and through a gorge whose slopes are thick with hardwood trees—is one of the loveliest in the state.

Park naturalists conduct walking tours into Donaldson Cave and also into **Bronson Cave.** At **Twin Caves** you can take a short ride on the underground river while a naturalist tells you about the tiny blind cavefish swimming beneath you. To reach the park go east on State Road 60 from Mitchell for about 3 miles; the park is on the north side of State Road 60—signs point the way. Contact Spring Mill State Park, P.O. Box 376, Mitchell 47446; (812) 849–4129.

131

Spring Mill Inn is a combination of rustic charm and modern conveniences. Constructed in 1939 of native limestone and remodeled in 1976, the buff-colored building is located in the heart of the park. Guest rooms are decorated with colonial furniture, and the dining room serves three meals a day. Dinner usually features cornsticks made from meal ground in the park. Swimming is a year-round activity in the unique indoor-outdoor pool. Rooms cost from $43.00 to $52.00 per night year-round, and roll-away cots are available for $5.00 each. Dinner prices range from $3.00 to $9.00, with breakfast and lunch considerably cheaper. Contact Spring Mill Inn, P.O. Box 68, Mitchell 47446; (812) 849–4081.

The greatest concentration of Indiana's several earthquake faults is located in Posey County in the southwestern corner of the state, but the longest fault occurs in south central Indiana. Known as the **Mt. Carmel Fault,** it extends 50 miles southeastward from the Morgan-Monroe county line into Washington County. One of the few places in the state where a fault can actually be seen on the surface of the land is alongside State Road 446, 2½ miles south of the Monroe-Lawrence county line, where ancient movements along the Mt. Carmel Fault have uplifted the land. (It may be reassuring for visitors—and nearby residents—to know that no movement of this fault has been recorded in the history of modern man.) For additional information visit the Indiana Geological Survey (IGS) at 611 North Walnut Grove Avenue in Bloomington, where detailed maps showing the location of the Mt. Carmel Fault are on open file. The IGS also can provide information about other faults in Indiana; it's open from 8:00 A.M. to 4:30 P.M. Monday through Friday; (812) 855–9350 or 855–7636.

MARTIN COUNTY

There's silver in them thar hills, if legend be truth! Since the first Europeans came to these parts, tales have abounded about the lost Indian treasure cave of **McBride's Bluffs.** For nearly one hundred years the Choctaw Indians lived in the bluffs area north of Shoals, taking shelter in one particular cave during severe weather. Absalom Shields, one of the first white settlers, told of the time when the Indians blindfolded him and took him to this cave, where he was shown a fabulous amount of silver crudely molded into bricks. Shortly after their disclosure to Shields, the Indians were forced to flee the area so hastily that they could not take the silver with them. They did, however, seal the entrance to the cave. When one of their tribe was later sent to claim the treasure, the trees he was to use as landmarks to guide him to the cave had been cleared away and he was never able to find the silver. Since then a few isolated bars of silver have been found above ground, but the whereabouts of the cave remains a secret to this day. It's not for lack of trying, though—people still search for the silver.

The precipitous cliffs known as McBride's Bluffs, which soar 175 feet above the East Fork of White River, are riddled with small caves. Because country roads may be unmarked, it's best to ask locally for exact directions to the bluffs, which lie approximately 5 miles north of Shoals and are shown on the official state highway map. Start out from Shoals going northwest on U.S. Highway 50/150, then turn north on State Road 450. Continue north to a side road about 1½ miles north of Dover Village and turn east toward White River; a single-lane gravel road winds along the riverbank at the base of the bluffs.

Martin County is one of the best places in the state for shunpiking (driving the backroads). Meandering country lanes lead past little-known havens of beauty—rugged hills, dense woodlands, sheer sandstone cliffs—that are even more beautiful when wildflowers color the spring landscape and trees don their autumn hues.

Jug Rock, a striking sandstone monolith that is the focal point of a state nature preserve, is a product of centuries of erosion. Although it stretches to a height of 60 feet and is more than 15 feet in diameter, it is difficult to see when the surrounding trees are heavy with foliage. The bottle-shaped rock stands on the north side of U.S. Highway 50/150 a little to the northwest of Shoals, about a mile beyond the White River bridge and some 200 yards downhill from the Shoals Overlook Rest Park. Stop at a small road-side pull-off on a high point along the highway and look for a large, flat slab that tops this unusual formation. To gain a better perspective of Jug Rock's dimensions, walk to its base along a 60-yard-long woodland path. For additional information contact the Division of Nature Preserves, Indiana Department of Natural Resources, 402 West Washington Street, Room W267, Indianapolis 46204; (317) 232–4052.

Directly west of Shoals you can see the bluffs of **Beaver Bend,** noted for the rare species of ferns that cling to the cliff and grow nearby. Beaver Bend is a sharp curve in the East Fork of White River where Beaver Creek flows into it. These cliffs reach their loftiest height at Spout Spring, where water emerges from a pipe driven into the solid rock wall. The honeycombed cliff that overhangs the spring is layered with ochre and yellow rocks that soar 400 feet into the air. Ask for directions locally; an old country road passes near the base of the bluffs.

A few miles downriver from Beaver Bend you can explore the picturesque **Hindostan Falls** area. In the early 1800s the thriving community of Hindostan stood on the banks of White River. It was abandoned in 1828, at the height of its prosperity, when a mysterious disease began killing its citizens. Only 6 feet high but nevertheless impressive, Hindostan Falls extends from one bank of the river to the other, creating scallops of white foam along the uneven path it follows. The power produced by the tremendous volume of water that passes over it each day was harnessed by the people of Hindostan to power their mills, while a large sandstone ledge below the falls provided the rock for the mill's foundations. Still evident today are the large square holes from which the rock was hewn, but the ledge is now used primarily by picnickers and fishermen looking for solitude. The pools below the falls teem with catfish, drum, crappie, white and smallmouth bass, buffalo, shad, and suckers. Officially designated a state fishing area, the site also offers a free concrete boat-launching ramp and some free primitive campsites. Do use caution here, though—the current is both strong and dangerous at times. To reach Hindostan Falls go south from Shoals on U.S. Highway 50/150 to State Road 550, turn west, and follow the signs to the falls area on the south side of State Road 550. Open at all times; free. Contact the Regional Access Manager, Public Access South, Hindostan Falls State Public Fishing Area, RR 2, Box 140, Montgomery 47558; (812) 644–7731.

Hoosier National Forest, just east of Hindostan Falls, occupies the southeast corner of Martin County. A drive along forest roads reveals a seemingly endless panorama of some of nature's most stunning handiwork: huge rock bluffs, woods, waterfalls, streams, and box canyons. For additional information contact Hoosier National Forest Headquarters, 811 Constitution Avenue, Bedford 47421; (812) 275–5987.

Northeast of Shoals, bordering the north side of U.S. Highway

50, is **Martin State Forest,** one of the nicest surprises in the state forest system. Within its 6,132 acres you can climb a fire tower, visit an arboretum, or tour one of five demonstration areas to learn about forest management practices. The most spectacular hike in the forest takes you over a rugged 3-mile trail that leads to Tank Spring, where water tumbles down 150 feet over moss-covered sandstone; come here in the spring when the greens are newborn and lustrous. Shady campsites atop a breezy ridge make this a great place to spend warm-weather days. Open at all times; free admission. Contact Martin State Forest, P.O. Box 599, Shoals 47581; (812) 247–3491.

If you happen through Loogootee, you might want to stop in at **Walker's Drug Company,** 200 John F. Kennedy Avenue. Quench your thirst at the soda fountain with a nickel Coca-Cola served in a six-ounce glass. If you think you can handle it, go for the 10- or 15-cent size. This is nostalgia we can all appreciate.

Owner Fintan Walker and his wife, Helen, have learned by hearsay that only two other establishments in the United States still sell Coca-Cola for its original 1940s price. (A Coca-Cola sales manager based in Evansville, Indiana, says he doesn't know of *any* others.) To add to the pleasure, the beverage is served in old-style Coca-Cola glasses, manufactured before the mid-1960s. The old style reads "Drink Coca-Cola" rather than the "Enjoy Coca-Cola" of later years. Walker's, founded in the 1870s, has been in the same family for three generations; (812) 295–2094.

Monroe County

Indiana University, which sits in the heart of Bloomington, enrolls nearly 33,000 students from all over the world. The diverse cultures they represent have given rise to a cuisine that is international in scope and truly extraordinary for a town this size (52,000 people, sans students). Eateries specialize in Irish, French, Greek, Mexican, German, Italian, Ethiopian, Middle Eastern, Malaysian, Indonesian, African, Thai, Tibetan, Japanese, and all styles of Chinese foods. Of course, American dishes and that staple of every college town in the country—pizza—are also available.

More than twenty pizza parlors thrive in Bloomington. One serves a pizza chosen by *People* magazine as the fourth best in the United States. You can try it for yourself at **Mother Bear's** (1428

East Third Street; 812–332–4495) or just down the street at **Bear's Place** (1316 East Third Street; 812–339–3460). The former is your basic pizzeria, just for eating; the latter serves pizza only after 4:45 P.M., but it offers big-screen television, a classic movies series, and live entertainment on the side. The sauce that brought Mother Bear's its fame is a bit on the spicy side, so arm yourself with lots of liquids.

Located on the second floor at 430 East Kirkwood Street (812–339–4295) is **The Wok,** a family-owned restaurant that offers authentic dishes in all four styles of Chinese cooking. Food is prepared using traditional recipes from the Orient, rather than the Americanized versions to which most of us are accustomed, and chopsticks are provided. Weather permitting, you can dine on the outside terrace. Open 11:00 A.M. to 9:30 P.M. Monday through Thursday, 11:00 A.M. to 10:00 P.M. Friday, noon to 10:00 P.M. Saturday, and noon to 9:00 P.M. Sunday. The Wok's authenticity was recently verified in a favorable review that appeared in *Ta Kung Pao,* the famous Hong Kong newspaper with a circulation of several million.

Located in a quaint old home at 412 East Sixth Street is a small cafe/restaurant known as **The Runcible Spoon,** where patrons can sit upstairs, downstairs, or outside in a Japanese garden. A 300-gallon aquarium occupies a dominant position on the main floor; more fish reside in a bathtub in the rest room. Jeff Danielson, the owner, likes to think that this relaxing atmosphere brings out the philosopher in everyone. The cuisine, ranging from Seoul barbeque to African groundnut soup to Indian mulligatawny, can only be described as eclectic. Freshly roasted gourmet coffee is the lifeblood of the cafe, luring a mix of customers that's as varied as the cuisine, and the homemade bagels produced in the in-house bakery are an exclusive in Bloomington. One thing diners won't find here is an ashtray, not even in the garden; the Runcible Spoon is a nonsmoking establishment. The restaurant is open 8:00 A.M. to 2:30 P.M. and 5:00 to 8:00 P.M. daily; the cafe is open 8:00 to 12:30 A.M. Monday through Saturday and 8:00 A.M. to 11:00 P.M. Sunday. The Spoon also serves a Sunday brunch; (812) 334–3997.

For gyros unsurpassed anywhere stop in at **The Trojan Horse** on the southeast corner of Kirkwood and Walnut streets. Paper-thin slices of beef and lamb are garnished with tomato slices, onion rings, and zaziki sauce, then served on pita. Have a Greek salad on the side, and top it all off with a Greek pastry. Open 11:00 A.M. to 11:00 P.M. Monday through Thursday; 11:00 A.M. to midnight Friday and Saturday; 3:00 to 9:00 P.M. Sunday; (812) 332–1101.

Before professional basketball player Michael Jordan soared with the National Basketball Association's Chicago Bulls, he soared with the 1984 gold-medal-winning U.S. Olympic basketball team. Since Indiana University's Bobby Knight served as the team's head coach that year, team trials were held in Bloomington. It didn't take long for Jordan to develop a taste for the **Peterson's** Smoothie, a taste he indulged every day he was in town. Years later, he recalled those days when he sent an autographed poster of himself to Jay Twomey, owner of Peterson's (a deli-style restaurant and bakery), with an inscription praising the Smoothie. Isaiah Thomas, no slouch at basketball himself, attended Indiana University and helped its basketball team win the 1981 NCAA championship before joining the NBA's Detroit Pistons. While an IU student, Thomas was such a devotee of the Smoothie that Peterson's staff let him stand behind the counter and make his own. Jordan and Thomas are not alone in their enthusiasm. Many IU graduates stop in for a Smoothie every time they return to campus because, they tell Twomey, it's the one thing they can't get anywhere else.

The fabled Smoothie is a fruit-flavored yogurt shake with a distinctive taste that Twomey achieves by using a special brand of low-fat frozen yogurt made in California. Not only is the shake a frosty, thirst-quenching delight that has been called Bloomington's favorite summertime drink, but it contains only half the calories and fat of milkshakes. Purchasers of Smoothies get their choice of yogurt flavors along with the fresh fruit and fruit juice they want blended with it. Peterson's, which is located at 1811 East Tenth Street in the Crosstown Shopping Center, is open 11:00 A.M. to 9:00 P.M. Tuesday through Sunday; (812) 336–5450.

Bloomington also boasts the **Snow Lion,** believed to be one of only two Tibetan restaurants in the country. (The other is in New York City.) The Bloomington restaurant, however, has a connection with Tibet that is one-of-a-kind. Jigme K. Norbu, who owns the Snow Lion, is the nephew of the Dalai Lama, the Buddhist priest-king who is Tibet's political and spiritual leader. Although

Norbu adjusts his recipes somewhat to appeal to the American palate (Tibetan food features plenty of liver, mutton, barley, and fat), he achieves an authentic Tibetan flavor by using traditional spices and herbs from Tibet. The menu includes such offerings as Phingtsel (beanthread sautéed with mixed vegetables), Thukpa Shamic (fried egg noodles sautéed with shrimp and vegetables), and Tasha Ngopa (Indian chicken curry with Tibetan seasonings served on a bed of rice). All entrées are served with a cup of Tibetan tea and a salad with a house dressing that's so popular, many people come here just to eat the salad. The only dessert offered is Deyse, a dish of steamed sweet rice with raisins that's topped with cold yogurt.

In addition to serving food, the restaurant introduces diners to the culture of Tibet. The Tibetan national flag, which features two snow lions grasping an iridescent jewel, hangs near the door. Tibetan music is interwoven with the classical selections that play softly in the background, and several Tibetan hand paintings representing good luck adorn the walls. The Snow Lion, located at 113 South Grant Street, also offers cuisine from other parts of the Orient; prices are moderate. Open for lunch from 11:30 A.M. to 2:00 P.M. Monday through Friday and for dinner from 5:00 to 10:00 P.M. daily; carryouts available all day. Call (812) 336–0835.

Generally known as the most religious country on earth, Tibet is a small, peace-loving nation that lies in a remote mountainous region along the southwestern border of China proper. Tibet has been intermittently governed by China through the centuries, last achieving independence in 1911. That status endured until 1950, when China once again asserted its rule. Since then some 1.2 million Tibetans have died in the struggle to regain their country's freedom, and the Dalai Lama has set up a government in exile in India. Thubten J. Norbu, a retired Indiana University professor who is the father of Jigme Norbu and the older brother of the Dalai Lama, was motivated by the plight of his homeland to found the **Tibetan Cultural Center** (TCC) in Bloomington. In 1987 the Dalai Lama came to Bloomington to consecrate the then-new ◆ **Jangchub Chorten,** the only Tibetan chorten in the United States and the cornerstone of the TCC. Rising 35 feet above its pastoral surroundings, the copper-topped, white, concrete monument to peace memorializes Tibetans who have died under Chinese rule. Sealed within the chorten are such religious artifacts as Buddhist scriptures, bits of clothing worn by ancient monks and saints, and hair clippings from thirteen Dalai Lamas (the current Dalai Lama is the fourteenth). The chorten, located on the TCC's twenty-acre property at 3655 South Snoddy Road, can be seen free of charge during daylight hours. A building near the chorten houses a museum, library, and workshop. For further information and a schedule of special cultural events sponsored by the TCC, contact the Center at P.O. Box 2581, Bloomington 47402; (812) 334–7046 or 855–8222.

Among the more unusual attractions on the Indiana University campus is the ◆ **Lilly Library of Rare Books and Manuscripts,** a repository of more than 400,000 books and 6 million manuscripts. Among its most recent acquisitions are the original scripts from the popular television show *Star Trek: The Next Generation.* (They also have scripts from the original *Star Trek.*) The library draws on its vast holdings to set up a series of changing exhibits throughout the year, but such treasures as a Gutenberg Bible, George Washington's letter accepting the presidency of the United States, Thomas Jefferson's copy of the Bill of Rights, four Shakespeare folios, and a major Lincoln collection are on permanent display. Free admission; open during the school year from 9:00 A.M. to 8:00 P.M. Monday through Thursday, 9:00 A.M. to 5:00 P.M. Friday and Saturday, and 1:00 to 5:00 P.M. Sunday (shorter hours during summer months). Call (812) 855–2452.

Although Indiana University's School of Music is famous throughout the world for its excellence, Bloomington-born songwriter Hoagy Carmichael earned a law degree here. Music was always his passion, however, and passion would eventually have its way. One night in 1926, while sitting alone on a spooning wall at the edge of campus thinking of the two girls then in his life, Carmichael looked up at the starry sky and began whistling a tune. Unable to get the song out of his mind, he dashed over to use the piano at a local hangout. A few minutes later the proprietor closed up and tossed Hoagy out. Fortunately for the world the song remained on Hoagy's mind—it ultimately became "Stardust."

When Hoagy died in 1981 at age eighty-two, he made his last trip home to be buried in Rose Hill Cemetery on Bloomington's west side. In 1986 Hoagy's family donated a large collection of the composer's memorabilia to Indiana University, and the school established a ◆ **Hoagy Carmichael Room** in which to display it. The composer's piano, a jukebox, photographs of Carmichael with numerous Hollywood stars, and the original manuscript of "Stardust," signed and dated by its composer on January 15, 1952, are just a few of the mementos visitors will see. Located in Room 006 of the **Archives of Traditional Music** in Morrison Hall, the Hoagy Carmichael Room is open free of charge by appointment. Other rooms of the archives—the largest university-based ethnographic sound archives in the country—house such varied holdings as tapes of 350 spoken languages from around the world, the music of the Tupi Indians of Brazil, and recordings of blues artists of the 1940s. The public is welcome to visit the archives and listen to its collections from 9:00 A.M. to 5:00 P.M. Monday through Friday; admission is free. Call the Hoagy Carmichael Room at (812) 855–4679 or the archives librarian at (812) 855–8631.

At the ◆ **Indiana University Cyclotron Facility** on Milo B. Sampson Lane at the campus's eastern edge, you can enter the world of nuclear physics. The variable-energy light-ion cyclotron is used by scientists from throughout the world to explore the mysteries of the atomic nucleus, as well as to conduct research concerning astrophysics and the application of space devices. A recent major upgrade equipped the facility with particle beams of unconventional and superior characteristics. If all this "tech talk" is a bit difficult to understand, the guides who lead free tours through the facility will be happy to clarify things. For a tour schedule call the facility at (812) 855–9365.

You can obtain more information about the attractions of Indiana University by contacting the Bloomington/Monroe County/Indiana University Visitors Center, 2855 North Walnut Street, Bloomington 47404; (812) 334–8900 or 1–800–800–0037.

If the campus looks familiar, it may be because you saw the award-winning movie *Breaking Away.* It was filmed in Bloomington and featured the university's **Little 500 Bicycle Race,** held here each spring. The swimming hole in the movie was one of the water-filled limestone quarries you can see in the surrounding countryside.

Seven miles north of Bloomington on State Road 37, **Oliver Winery,** Indiana's oldest and largest, offers a free tour, free wine tasting, and, on Saturday evenings in June and July, outdoor concerts (most of which are free) on the parklike grounds. Owner Bill

Oliver, a law professor at Indiana University, started his vineyards in 1971 and now produces 40,000 gallons of wine a year. Several of the fifteen or so varieties have won gold and silver medals in competitions throughout the country. If you're in the mood for lunch, you can have "a jug of wine, a loaf of bread," and your own "thou" beside you at a picnic table outside or at a table in the cozy tasting room inside. Cheeses, summer sausage, fruits, popcorn, maple syrup, and unique limestone gifts are also available. Open 10:00 A.M. to 6:00 P.M. Monday through Saturday and noon to 6:00 P.M. Sunday; closes at 8:00 P.M. Friday and Saturday in June and July and at 5:00 P.M. daily January through March; tours available Saturday and Sunday or by appointment. Contact Oliver Wine Co., Inc., 8024 North State Road 37, Bloomington 47404; (812) 876–5800.

Morgan-Monroe State Forest wanders over 23,916 acres, most of which occupy northeastern Monroe County. Nestled in a clearing in the midst of the woods is a rustic log cabin where a true get-away-from-it-all experience awaits you. **Draper's Cabin** is described by the state as primitive, and the description is apt. There's no electricity, all water has to be carried in, heat is provided by a stone fireplace, and you make your bed on the floor. The forest provides plenty of wood for the fireplace, but it's up to you to gather it and carry it in. Only dead material can be used, and no saws are allowed. You can cook in the fireplace or, if you bring your own grill, on a concrete slab outdoors. The cabin contains nary a stick of furniture, but two picnic tables are just outside the door. A few yards away a small stream sometimes trickles by and sometimes doesn't—it depends on the rainfall.

Draper's Cabin is the only such cabin on any state-owned land, and you can rent the whole thing for $10.50 a night, including tax. The maximum stay is fourteen days. Available by advance reservation from April to November through the Property Manager, Morgan-Monroe State Forest, 6220 Forest Road, Martinsville 46151; (317) 342–4026.

To reach the forest go north from Bloomington on State Road 37 to Forest Road, the main entrance road, which runs east off of State Road 37 into the forest just before you reach the Morgan-Monroe county line. If you go in the spring or fall, you probably won't be able to resist a hike through the woods. Brochures for the trails, which include 9- and 7-mile loops and a ¾-mile pathway through the **Scout Ridge State Nature Preserve,** are available at the office building. If you do your walking during hunting season, it's best to wear bright colors.

ORANGE COUNTY

When Larry Bird first burst on the professional basketball scene in 1979, he was promptly dubbed "the hick from French Lick," by many sportswriters across the nation. Larry Bird went on to establish himself as the very heart of the Boston Celtics, and the sports world learned two things: He sure could play basketball, and, shyness and Hoosier dialect aside, he was no hick. What's more, Bird's hometown of French Lick, although small, is also the home of one of the most luxurious all-season resorts in the nation.

French Lick came into being because of some rich mineral springs that flowed from the hillsides. In 1837, to accommodate the hordes of people who flocked here to "take the waters," the French Lick Springs Hotel opened. Around the turn of the century, the hotel was purchased by Thomas Taggart, a nationally known political figure who served as mayor of Indianapolis and as U.S. senator from Indiana. Taggart, who juggled his two careers, was named chairman of the National Democratic Party in 1904. His national prominence came at a time when spas were at the height of their popularity, and the elite of society and politics from all over the country descended on French Lick to drink the waters from its springs and to partake of the mineral baths.

Gambling was added, luring even more visitors, including both celebrities and gangsters. In 1932 several state governors met here and decided to back Franklin Delano Roosevelt for president. The Vanderbilts, Morgans, and Whitneys came here to play, followed later by such stars as Lana Turner, Roy Rogers, Dale Evans, and Gene Autry.

Today the gambling is long since gone, and the opulent era of the spas has drawn to a close. But the hotel, as lovely as ever with its tall white pillars, crystal chandeliers, and plush carpeting, still operates as the **French Lick Springs Resort.** It stands in the midst of 2,600 acres of hills, woodlands, landscaped lawns, and formal gardens, a gracious queen who has splendidly survived the test of time. Although the springs are still there, guests come today to relax in the peaceful setting and to enjoy a full range of activities—golf on two eighteen-hole courses, tennis on indoor or outdoor courts, two swimming pools (one indoors for year-round use), skeet and trap shooting, horseback riding, bicycling, and such games as bowling, shuffleboard, badminton, volleyball, horseshoes, and miniature golf. There's even a modern-day version of the spa—a health and fitness center. From approximately December to March, you can go skiing on six nearby slopes or skate on the hotel's ice rink.

As impressive as it all is, what you'll most likely remember as much as anything is the food served at Chez James, the resort's gourmet restaurant. Such delights as New England codfish cakes, Spanish omelets, braised capon, South African lobster tail, peach Melba, strawberries Romanoff, and baked Alaska Vesuvius may appear on the menu, along with favorite Hoosier foods. The hotel's six other restaurants serve a variety of food in more casual surroundings.

Most facilities, many special activities, and transportation to and from French Lick Airport are included in the rates, which range from $150 to $225 per night for two people (breakfast and dinner included). There are also seasonal rates and many special packages. Contact French Lick Springs Resort, State Road 56, French Lick 47432; (812) 936-9300 or 1-800-457-4042.

Railroad buffs will be intrigued by the ◆ **Indiana Railway Museum,** located just north of French Lick Springs Resort's parking lot on State Road 56. Operated as a nonprofit corporation, the museum has its headquarters in the old Monon Railroad station, where several steam locomotives, a rare railway post office car, and a 1951 dining car are among the memorabilia on display. Visitors can also board the **French Lick, West Baden & Southern Railway** for a 1¾-hour, 20-mile, round-trip ride between French Lick and Cuzco, Indiana. A diesel locomotive pulls 1920s-era passenger cars away from the station and plunges into the wooded terrain of Hoosier National Forest, offering its passengers views of rugged Orange County backcountry where no roads penetrate. Along the way the train passes through a 2,200-foot tunnel, one of Indiana's longest. Children are especially delighted by the train robberies staged on holiday and various other weekends. Trains depart at 10:00 A.M., 1:00 P.M., and 4:00 P.M. each Saturday, Sunday, and holiday April through November. For additional information write the Indiana Railway Museum,

143

Box 150, French Lick 47432; or call (812) 936–2405 or 1–800–748–7246.

The museum also operates a 2-mile round-trip trolley ride between French Lick and West Baden. At the latter, visitors see all that remains of the ◆ **West Baden Hotel.** The architectural masterpiece, once known as the "most unique hotel on earth" and the "Carlsbad of America," was world-famous in the early 1900s, but through the years it did not fare as well as French Lick's resort.

Begun in October 1901, construction on the West Baden Hotel was completed 8½ months later—an astonishing accomplishment in any day but truly extraordinary given the technology of the time. Its imaginative owner, Colonel Lee Sinclair, had conjured up visions of a sumptuous hotel that established architects of the day said was impossible to build. Urged on by his daughter Lillian, Colonel Sinclair finally found an enterprising young architect who accepted the challenge not only to build the hotel but to do so for $414,000—with a $100-a-day penalty clause if construction took longer than the agreed-on 200 working days.

When finished, the dome above the immense central atrium, larger than the dome at St. Peter's Cathedral in Rome, was regarded as the "eighth wonder of the world." Two hundred feet in diameter, 130 feet above the floor, ribbed with 24 steel girders mounted on rollers to accommodate expansion and contraction, it remained the world's largest self-supporting dome until the Houston Astrodome was completed in 1965. The atrium floor was covered with 12 million Italian marble tiles, and the elaborate sunken gardens were planted with rare flowers from Europe and the Orient. Circling the atrium and its gardens were 708 guest rooms on six floors.

West Baden Hotel thrived for thirty years, attracting an illustrious clientele that included General John J. Pershing, J. M. Studebaker, and Diamond Jim Brady, as well as the likes of Al Capone. In 1932, however, it became a casualty of the Great Depression.

Subsequently it served as winter headquarters for the old Hagenbach-Wallace Circus, as a Jesuit school, and as the home of Northwood Institute, a college that trained its students for employment in the hotel restaurant field. During the Jesuits' tenancy the face of the old hotel was altered forever. Some of the grander touches, they felt, were unseemly for their austere lifestyle. And so the

144

Roman-style baths were wrecked and hauled away, the gardens were left untended, the lavish furniture was sold, the beautiful Moorish towers were removed from the roof, and the arabesque brickwork atop the building was straightened. Unfortunately the hotel has deteriorated badly in recent years but an exterior view of the great dome still inspires awe. Funds are currently being sought to restore the one-of-a-kind building that is now designated a National Historic Landmark and one of the United State's ten most endangered historic places. At this writing visitors may tour the atrium on weekends, but they must pay a nominal admission fee (and sign a waiver of liability in case the walls come tumbling down). For up-to-date information contact the French Lick/West Baden Chamber of Commerce, P.O. Box 347, French Lick 47432; (812) 936–2405.

Kimball International manufactures pianos at its plant on State Road 56 in West Baden Springs, and visitors can watch master craftsmen assemble upright and grand pianos through all phases of the operation, from stringing to final tuning. It's a unique experience that's free of charge, but make your arrangements at least two weeks in advance. Contact Kimball International, P.O. Box 432, French Lick 47432; (812) 936–4522 or (800) 422–1611. The tours are offered at 1:30 P.M. each working day to groups of ten or more, but you may be able to join an existing tour. If summer heat is a problem for you, you should know that the 300,000-square-foot plant has a concrete floor and no air-conditioning.

No visit to Orange County would be complete without a stop at Punkin Center, 8 miles southeast of Orleans in the heart of the county's Amish country. The tiny hamlet is listed on the official state road map as Pumpkin Center, but don't you believe it. The late Add Gray always said so, and since he lived here all his life, he should know.

On Halloween Day in 1922, Add opened the ❖ **Punkin Center General Store** with $327.28 worth of groceries he'd purchased from a wholesaler in Orleans. That store evolved into **Add's Museum of All Sorts of Stuff**—a combination home, general store, and barn—which now is presided over by Add's charming widow, Mabel. Although the general store is no longer open for business, it is still a repository for many of the Grays' relics and antiques. Swords, bells, plates (both dining and upper),

145

saddles, sleighs, wagons, a crank-style telephone and the opera-tor's switchboard, Colorado sagebrush, Indiana tickleweed, Span-ish moss, Utah tumbleweed, a baby casket, an antique baseball uniform, an old-fashioned soda fountain, a roulette wheel, several scarecrows, a cast-iron chandelier from a Louisville, Kentucky, funeral home, a spring-operated churn, a collection of Indiana license plates that date back to 1913 (including the only one ever made in the state with the number 1,000,000), a wooden Santa Claus suspended from the barn roof who waves his hand and jin-gles some sleigh bells at the flick of a switch—this list just skims the surface. Add, who claimed he hadn't thrown anything away since 1917, gave new meaning to the phrase "pack rat."

When you arrive at Punkin Center, you might spot a sign that says COME ON IN. WE WERE EXPECTING YOU. EVERYTHING ELSE HAS GONE WRONG TODAY. Ignore it. It's just Add's delightful sense of humor at work. Although Add is gone now, Mabel likes nothing better than to welcome visitors and show them through the mind-boggling accumulation of goods.

Be sure to ask Mabel about the yarns Add used to spin—yarns about folks like old Ma Hollis, for instance, who made wine and beer for the local farmers and occasionally took a few swigs her-self. When Pa Hollis died suddenly, she said he fell and hit his head on the pine floor—but it was hickory bark they found in his forehead. Or Rough Tedrow, who could shinny up a tree and catch a coon bare-handed. During the Great Depression he charged traveling salesmen 10 cents to watch him catch snapping turtles by the head. The biggest night in Punkin Center's history occurred in 1926, when Ray Trinkle dropped by the store carrying a lighted lantern and walked a mite too close to the gas tank. And many's the night the local folk stopped in to watch Bob McCoy spit on the store's potbellied stove from clear across the room. His accuracy was uncanny.

The Punkin Center museum is open most anytime Mabel is home. Take State Road 56 east from Paoli to a narrow, black-topped lane known as Potato Road (the locals call it Tater Road). Take Potato Road north for about 2 miles, cross a bridge over Stamper Creek, and you'll be in Punkin Center. Follow these direc-tions carefully, for there are two Pumpkin Centers shown on the Indiana map—the other one lies just a few miles to the east in adjoining Washington County. Mabel's mailing address is 2197

North County Road 500E, Orleans 47452; (812) 723–2432.

Although the name Punkin Center conjures up pictures of Halloween, you might want to journey here in the spring and make a visit to Orleans at the same time. Orleans has been the official **Dogwood Capital of Indiana** since 1970, a few years after Mr. and Mrs. C. E. Wheeler started planting dogwood trees along State Road 37, one of the town's main thoroughfares. It was a labor of love for the Wheelers, who believed that the dogwood's pink and white blooms had no equal for beauty. Today the trees cover a 12-mile stretch between Mitchell on the north and Paoli on the south, and more trees are added each year in what is now a communitywide project. They're usually in full bloom in late April and early May.

Orange County is also the site of two of the Hoosier State's most unusual natural landmarks. On the southern edge of Orangeville, which lies about 7 miles southwest of Orleans via country roads, you can view the **Orangeville Rise of the Lost River.** An underground river surfaces here as an artesian spring, flowing from a cave into a 220-foot-wide rock-walled pit at the base of a limestone bluff. The three-acre preserve is well marked, and there's a pull-off for parking. For additional information contact The Nature Conservancy, Indiana Field Office, 1330 West Thirty-eighth Street, Indianapolis 46208; (317) 923–7547.

Not far from Paoli, on the edge of Hoosier National Forest, is an eighty-acre tract of virgin woodland known as ◆ **Pioneer Mothers Memorial Forest,** whose magnificent trees are from 150 to 600 years old. Its crown jewel is the Walnut Cathedral, a moist cove that, according to the U.S. Department of the Interior, contains the finest black walnut trees of their kind in the entire country. From Paoli go south on State Road 37 for about 1¼ miles to the Pioneer Mothers State Wayside on the east side of the road. From this picnic area you can follow marked trails for a short distance into the Memorial Forest. Contact the Forest Supervisor, Hoosier National Forest, 811 Constitution Avenue, Bedford 47421; (812) 275–5987.

OWEN COUNTY

The ◆ **Barn House,** a 70-foot-tall, 135-foot-long structure that defies description, rises from a hillside near Vandalia and regularly startles passersby. Begun in 1972 and completed a decade later, the house is a monument to recycling. James Pendleton, its builder, razed eleven barns and seven houses to collect the materials he needed to construct his one-of-a-kind house. Its thirty-two rooms, no two of which are the same shape or size and no two of which are perpendicular to each other, contain more than 7,200 square feet of floor space. Access to the rooms is provided by fifteen stairways and ladders, with a few hidden passageways thrown in for good measure. Rising five levels in some places and four levels in others, the unique house also features seventy-four different roof angles and twin rooftop towers. Pendleton, who once lived in the house but now occupies a smaller residence on the same property, is happy to give tours of the Barn House to anyone who stops by when he's at home. On the average, that adds up to about twenty persons per week. Pendleton's guest book reveals that his visitors have come not only from this country but from such faraway places as Russia, Czechoslovakia, Thailand, Vietnam, India, and Japan. Each year on the first weekend of October, he hosts a festival at his home that's highlighted by Barn House tours. To reach the Barn House, go west from Vandalia on State Road 46 for about 4 miles to Bixler Road, and turn south (just before you come to Bixler Road, you'll pass the Garrard Chapel Church on the left side of State Road 46); the Barn House is the second house on the right (west) side of Bixler Road. You'll have no trouble recognizing the house once you see it, but since Bixler Road can be difficult to identify, you may want to inquire locally. James Pendleton has no phone, but you can write to him at RR 1, Bowling Green 47833.

PARKE COUNTY

All of Parke County is a museum of **covered bridges.** Within its boundaries are more covered bridges than you'll find in any other county in the United States—more, in fact, than you'll find in most states. At last count, thirty-two of them remained intact. What's more, they're all authentic, with the two oldest dating back to 1856 and the youngster of the bunch to 1920. All thirty-two were placed on the National Register of Historic Sites in 1978.

Joe Sturm, a retired farmer and carpenter, has served as official bridge inspector for more than twelve years and can relate all kinds of interesting facts about them. He can tell you, for instance, that so many bridges were built because of the numerous zigzagging streams in the country, that the only metal used in constructing them is the bolts, and that the bridge at Mecca was built on dry ground and a nearby stream rerouted to pass under it.

Most of the bridges still support traffic, and the folks in Parke County have mapped out four automobile routes that provide access to most of them. A free map outlining each route is available at the Parke County Tourist Information Center, located in the old train depot on U.S. Highway 36 at the eastern edge of Rockville. It's open 9:00 A.M. to 4:00 P.M. daily Memorial Day weekend to the first weekend of November, and Monday through Saturday the rest of the year; (317) 569–5226.

The northwest route leads you to West Union Bridge, at 315 feet the longest in the county. The community of Bridgeton, with its many unusual shops, is a highlight of the southernmost route. Standing on the bank of Big Raccoon Creek, next to the double-span Bridgeton Bridge, is the Weise Mill. It's been grinding meal since it was built in 1823, making it the oldest known gristmill west of the Allegheny Mountains that's still in service. Directly west of Rockville is the Sim Smith Bridge, which claims the distinction of being the county's only haunted bridge.

If you head northeast from Rockville, you'll come to **Turkey Run State Park,** noted for its steep ravines, its sandstone formations, and the **Rocky Hollow-Falls Canyon State Nature Preserve,** which protects a lush primeval forest. The **Narrows Bridge,** one of the most photographed in the county, crosses Sugar Creek in the park. A tree-shaded inn in the park offers overnight accommodations in fifty-two rooms and twenty-one nearby cabins, two swimming pools, and four tennis courts; call (317) 597–2211. Write Turkey Run State Park, Route 1, Box 164, Marshall 47859, or phone (317) 597–2635.

On U.S. Highway 41 north of Rockville, just before you reach the state park, stands **Gobbler's Knob Country Store,** where you can purchase nostalgic wares that revive memories of grandmother—penny candies in jars, pickles from a barrel, sassafras bark, country hams, sunbonnets, corncob jelly, and carnival glass; (317) 597–2558.

Follow U.S. Highway 36 east from Rockville for 1 mile, and cross Billie Creek Bridge into a turn-of-the-century village and

149

Covered Bridge in Parke County

farmstead where the crafts and skills of yesteryear are on vivid display. One of the finest living museums in the state, ◆ **Billie Creek Village** is open daily from mid-January to late December; hours vary. An admission fee is charged when craftsmen are in residence (generally Saturday, Sunday, holidays, and during the Covered Bridge Festival in October); admission free at other times. Write Billie Creek Village, RR 2, Box 27, Rockville 47872; (317) 569–3430.

Parke County originally had more than fifty covered bridges, but several were lost to fire, flood, and natural deterioration before a preservation effort was begun. Each October since 1957, the county has celebrated its heritage with a ten-day **Covered Bridge Festival.** The nationally recognized event regularly lures some 500,000 visitors.

Another popular festival is the late-winter **Maple Fair,** which takes place when local sugar camps are producing maple syrup.

For more information contact Parke County, Inc., P.O. Box 165, Rockville 47872; (317) 569–5226.

PERRY COUNTY

Besides its bountiful natural beauty, this Ohio River county is worth visiting for its array of unusual monuments.

If Tell City has a trademark, it is the life-size **statue of William Tell** and his son that serves as the centerpiece for the fountain in front of city hall. The statue is a reflection of the town's Swiss heritage and a tribute to the legendary Swiss hero from whom Tell City took its name. Town residents were delighted when, in 1974, plans were announced for the construction of the fountain that would honor the town's namesake, but they never dreamed it would cause such a fuss.

After the statue had been formed by Evansville sculptor Don Ingle, it was sent to a New York foundry to be cast in bronze. Ingle and his wife then personally picked up the 500-pound statue in New York, placed it in a rented U-Haul van, and headed home for the formal dedication. Imagine their horror when, after spending the night in an Ohio motel, they discovered that the van—statue and all—had been stolen as they slept. Everyone got into the act, with local police and the FBI cooperating in a frantic search and news media throughout the country warning everyone to be on the lookout for the kidnapped William Tell. The nationwide furor was such that the thief eventually abandoned his ill-gotten gain on a side street in Cleveland, and the statue was escorted the rest of the way home without further ado. You can see William Tell today in his place of honor atop the fountain—one arm holding his crossbow, the other arm around his son's shoulder, and not an apple in sight.

Poised above State Road 66 near Troy, a towering 19-foot statue of Christ overlooks the Ohio River, arms extended in an eternal blessing of all who gaze on it. Herbert Jogerst, a German artist, sculpted the statue when he was a prisoner-of-war in Indiana during World War II. It stands on a bluff once owned by Robert Fulton, of steamboat fame, and is now part of a summer camp for crippled children. Illuminated at night, the all-white **Christ of the Ohio** is always visible to travelers on land or water.

At St. Augustine's Church in Leopold stands the **Shrine of**

Our Lady of Consolation, whose strange history dates back to the Civil War. Three young Union Army soldiers from Perry County, members of the church, were confined in the infamous prison at Andersonville, Georgia. They vowed to one another that if they lived through the horror of that experience they would donate a shrine to their church as a token of their gratitude. Miraculously they all survived, and one of them personally made a trip to Belgium to oversee the making of an exact reproduction of a shrine he remembered seeing in a small village church there.

Some historians claim that, unable to obtain the reproduction he desired, the young man stole the original and transported it back to Indiana, sparking an international incident between the governments of the two countries. It happened, however, that Leopold had been named for the Leopold who was then king of Belgium, who was so pleased to learn of his namesake that he allowed the shrine to remain there. It can be seen today, a statue of Mary and the infant Jesus, each wearing a white gown, a blue robe, and a crown of jewels. Call (812) 843–5143 for information.

One of the Hoosier State's finest historical landmarks is now a vast and silent structure—the huge, castlelike **Cannelton Cotton Mill.** From 1849 until 1965 the mill was a beehive of activity. Once the busiest industry in Indiana, it contained the most modern textile machinery, rivaling the better-known mills of New England. Some 400 laborers operating 372 looms spun raw cotton into thread and cloth, and a good worker in the old days could sometimes earn as much as $4.50 a day. Union Army uniforms were made here during the Civil War.

Often honored for its architecture and described as one of the most outstanding engineering feats of its time in the Midwest, the mammoth stone structure is 60 feet wide by 280 feet long and has 5-foot-thick interior walls. Two copper-roofed towers, each more than 100 feet tall, serve as landmarks for Ohio River traffic. One of the towers held water that could be used to flood each of the five floors in case of fire, a constant threat in a cotton mill. The second tower, besides serving as a fire escape, was designed to reduce the risk of fire; it contained five trapdoors that were opened twice each working day so that air could be drawn down through a chimney to remove accumulated lint.

It is a gaunt gray ghost now, but people still come—to view the mill from the road, to marvel at its unusual style, to photograph a treasured relic of the past that has outlived its days of glory. For information about tours of the mill, located on Washington Street in Cannelton, contact the Perry County Chamber of Commerce, 123 Main Street, P.O. Box 82, Tell City 47586; (812) 547–2385.

Back in Tell City tour the ◈ **Tell City Pretzel Company,** which may be the only one in the United States and one of the few in the world that still produces pretzels the original way—by handtwisting them. A Swiss baker brought the recipe with him from Europe when he settled here more than one hundred years ago. Although the recipe is still a secret, passed down from owner to owner, visitors are welcome to watch the twisters at work each Monday through Friday from 7:00 A.M. until about 3:00 P.M. The 12,000 pretzels produced daily are sold on the premises and by mail order. Contact Tell City Pretzels, 632 Main Street, Tell City 47586; (812) 547–4631.

POSEY COUNTY

In 1814 a group of German Lutheran separatists migrated westward from Pennsylvania to the verdant valley of Wabash River. There they purchased some 30,000 acres of land along the riverbank and carved from the dense woodlands the personification of a dream—a tiny communal settlement they named Harmony. An industrious people, the Harmonists established a variety of successful industries that ranged from the making of fine silks to the distilling of whiskey, and their products were much in demand throughout the eastern United States. They developed prefabricated houses, dug tunnels beneath them, and used the cool air therein to air-condition their dwellings. Oranges were grown year-round in their greenhouses. Eventually they found themselves with enough leisure time to start bickering among themselves, and in 1825 their leader, Father George Rapp, sold the entire town to Robert Owen, a wealthy industrialist from Scotland.

Owen envisioned a utopia of a different sort, a commune that focused on innovative education and intellectual pursuits. His ◈ **New Harmony** lured scientists, artists, writers, and social reformers whose ideas and creations made a lasting impact on our country's history. America's first free public school system, kindergarten, day-care center, free library, trade school, women's

153

club, and civic dramatic club came to fruition here. One of Owen's sons became an eminent geologist and was commissioned to make the first survey of new government lands in the West. After that son was appointed U.S. Geologist in 1938, he ran the U.S. Geological Survey from New Harmony for seventeen years. Another of Owen's sons entered Congress, became an early crusader for the rights of women, and drafted the legislation that established the Smithsonian Institution. Yet another son became president of Indiana's Purdue University. Although many of the concepts developed at Owen's New Harmony have survived, the commune foundered in 1827. One reason for this was that its inhabitants did not possess the husbandry skills needed to feed its populace. While lofty ideas and ideals were being discussed inside, the hogs were invading the vegetables outside.

New Harmony was never deserted, however. Its reputation as an intellectual center gradually faded, but many residents stayed on, putting down roots that have kept the community alive to this day.

In the 1940s Jane Owen, wife of a direct descendant of Robert Owen, visited here and was so entranced by what she saw that she initiated a restoration project. Today New Harmony is a state historical site, and people come from all over the country to take a twelve-point tour that traces the history of the settlement from its original log cabins to some striking structures added in recent years.

Enclosed within the brick walls of the Harmonist cemetery at the west end of Granary Street are more than 200 unmarked graves—symbolic of continued equality in death—and several Indian burial mounds. The Labyrinth, a fascinating maze of paths and hedges on the south edge of town, represents the twists and turns and choices that confront each of us in our passage through life.

Completed in 1979, the ultramodern stark white Atheneum that rises from a meadow near the riverbank has garnered many honors for its architectural design. The visitor center within periodically shows a film entitled *The New Harmony Experience* and exhibits a scale model of the original town; (812) 682–4474.

Serving as the altar for the Roofless Church, a paved courtyard that's open to the sky, is a unique dome that's shaped like an inverted rosebud but casts the shadow of a full-blown rose. Its design was inspired by writer George Sand, who remarked that the sky was the only roof vast enough to embrace all of worshiping humanity. When he visited here in 1963, Paul Tillich, the world-renowned philosopher and theologian, was so impressed by the Roofless Church that he said it alone justified our century. When Tillich died not long afterward, his ashes were buried in Tillich Park opposite the church.

One of the most beautiful sights at New Harmony, however, is a seasonal event orchestrated by nature. The first golden raintree in the nation was planted at New Harmony, and today there is scarcely a lawn or street anywhere in town that does not boast at least one of these lovely trees. An ornamental tree that originated in the Orient, the golden raintree is unusually beautiful throughout the year but is most glorious around the third week in June when it bursts into full bloom, then sheds its petals in a virtual shower of brilliant gold. There's no place in the United States where this tree grows in greater quantity, and New Harmony celebrates its beauty each June with a festival.

New Harmony is easily explored on foot. Historic New Harmony, Inc., has its headquarters at 506½ Main Street and offers general information as well as guided tours for nominal fees; contact the organization at P.O. Box 579, New Harmony 47631; (812) 682–4488.

Even the town's commercial district has a revitalized turn-of-the-century aura, and although it's not historic, the redbrick **New Harmony Inn** is a charming mix of traditional and modern design that blends well with its surroundings. Wood-burning fireplaces, rush-seated rockers, kitchenettes, living rooms, and spiral staircases that lead to sleeping lofts are all available. Trees march right up to glass walls that enclose a heated pool, and the sky is always visible through a sliding glass roof. The beautifully landscaped grounds share the shoreline of a placid lake with open fields and patches of forest laced with biking and hiking paths. Rates vary seasonally. Contact the New Harmony Inn, 508 North Street, P.O. Box 581, New Harmony 47631; (812) 682–4491.

Next door, a gourmet restaurant, the **Red Geranium,** serves lunch and dinner six days a week. The spinach salad with house dressing, warm homemade bread, and Shaker lemon pie are really special. Children's menus are available. Hours are 11:00 A.M. to 10:00 P.M. Tuesday through Thursday, 11:00 A.M. to 11:00 P.M. Friday and Saturday, and 11:00 A.M. to 8:00 P.M. Sunday; closed Monday and some major holidays; (812) 682–4431.

By driving south from New Harmony on State Road 69 for about 24 miles, almost to the Ohio River, you are suddenly confronted with a scene that might have been transported here from the Deep South. **Hovey Lake** resembles a southern swamp, particularly in the slough areas to the east of the lake. Its waters are studded with huge bald cypress trees—one noteworthy old patriarch has lived to about 250 years of age. Along the lakeshore are southern red oak, wild pecans, mistletoe, holly, and swamp privet.

Birdwatchers spot great blue herons, American egrets, double-breasted cormorants, and pileated woodpeckers. Osprey have been known to nest here, and white ibis, bald eagles, hawks, and owls frequent the area. In the autumn, usually beginning in the first week in October, some 500,000 ducks and geese arrive for the winter.

Hovey Lake, formed about 500 years ago, is an oxbow lake that occupies an old channel of the nearby Ohio River. It's now part of a 4,300-acre state fish and wildlife area, but even if you don't like to fish, you can rent a rowboat, glide among the majestic trees that rise from the surface of the water, and enjoy the serenity and seclusion of this lovely place. When seen through the mists of early morning, Hovey Lake takes on the aura of a dream.

Close to the launching ramp, you'll find an oak-shaded picnic area and forty-eight primitive campsites. Contact Hovey Lake State Fish and Wildlife Area, 1298 West Graddy Road, Mt. Vernon 47620; (812) 838–2927.

PUTNAM COUNTY

In the valley of Big Walnut Creek lies one of the most beautiful and unusual natural areas in Indiana. The clear waters of the creek calmly meander southward through steep ravines studded with limestone outcroppings. A great blue heron rookery that has been continuously occupied for more than sixty years shares the forest with the great horned owl and more than 120 other species of birds. What is thought to be the largest sugar maple in the world, as well as the two largest sassafras trees and the second biggest hemlock in Indiana, thrive within the preserve's confines. Located about 1½ miles northeast of Bainbridge, the **Big Walnut State**

Nature Preserve lies primarily along that part of the creek between Pine Bluff Covered Bridge and Rolling Stone Covered Bridge. It's open daily, free of charge, during daylight hours. For additional information and exact directions, contact The Nature Conservancy, Indiana Field Office, 1330 West Thirty-eighth Street, Indianapolis 46208; (317) 923–7547; or the Greencastle Chamber of Commerce, P.O. Box 389, Greencastle 46135; (317) 653–4517.

Roachdale, a small village in the northern part of the county, is the site of one of the zaniest events held anywhere—an **annual race for cockroaches.** Each Fourth of July contestants adorned with brightly colored racing stripes line up in their appointed lanes atop a plywood course and await the official signal to start. Entrants with a tendency to wander at this critical time are kept in place with flypaper. At last someone calls out, in true Indianapolis 500 fashion, "Gentlemen and ladies! Start your cockroaches!" and the race is on. The rules permit owners to place edible enticements behind the finish line, and that's usually all a cockroach with any get-up-and-go needs to spur it on its way.

The rules are simple—any trainer with a live roach may enter. And how, you might ask, do you train a roach? One woman claims she taught her bug to do isometrics.

It's not unusual to see racers from faraway states, but recently the contest went international. One woman hand-carried her roach—a thoroughbred—all the way from England. It didn't win, but the officials ran up a British flag in its honor.

If you have a roach that's into racing or if you'd just like more information, contact Jim Holland, Roachdale Lions Club, RR 1, Box 110, Roachdale 46172; (317) 522–4244.

SPENCER COUNTY

Poised majestically atop a hill, the ◆ **St. Meinrad Archabbey** emerges unexpectedly from the trees and hills of northeastern Spencer County. Your eyes are first drawn to the soaring twin spires of the Abbey Church, then to the entire complex of beautiful buildings that house a theological school, a college, a monastery, and such income-producing enterprises as a publishing company, a winery, and a meat-packing plant.

When the abbey was founded by immigrant missionaries from Switzerland in 1854, the monks themselves transported the sandstone from a quarry 1 mile distant, hand-chipped it into the desired shape, and erected buildings patterned after the European medieval style so vivid in their memories. Newer, more modern buildings appear among the old ones these days, but all interiors remain starkly simplistic in keeping with the order's dedication to a spiritual rather than materialistic lifestyle.

Visitors who roam the well-maintained grounds find themselves in the company of priests and brothers in simple black gowns—teachers, lay employees, and some 400 students who are training for the priesthood. Although silence is part of the Benedictine life, it is expected only from 9:00 P.M. through breakfast the following day and at all times in the halls of the monastery. Otherwise, the monks and brothers are fun-loving, hospitable people who enjoy conversing with visitors. There's even a campus

St. Meinrad Archabbey

bar and pizzeria called The Unstable that's open two hours each weekday night and three hours on weekends.

You can join the monks for a worship service; Mass is in English. Brochures for self-guided tours can be picked up at the Guest House Office from 9:00 A.M. to 4:00 P.M. Monday through Saturday and 1:00 to 4:00 P.M. Sunday. Free guided tours are available by advance appointment; contact St. Meinrad Archabbey, St. Meinrad 47577; (812) 357–6611. The abbey is located on State Road 62, just south of I–64, near the Perry-Spencer county line; follow the signs.

Two notable residents have made their homes in this county, and it would be tough to decide who is more famous—unless you are six years old or younger.

The U.S. Postal Service receives several million pieces of mail each Christmas addressed to Santa Claus, and it's all forwarded to Santa Claus's true domicile—a small town in southern Indiana. A few million more letters and packages are sent to the local postmaster with the request that they be stamped with the ❖ **Santa Claus, Indiana,** postmark before being sent on to their final destinations. Pretty heady stuff for a town with a population of about 500, give or take a few elves.

Although the town has borne its unusual name since 1852, it became world-famous only after Robert Ripley featured it in his *Believe It or Not* column in 1929. Such a hullabaloo followed that the annual Town Christmas Party had to be rescheduled for early October, when there was time to deal with such things. Today the **Santa Claus Post Office,** whose stone front resembles a castle, probably gets more visitors than any other post office in the country. Folks can't believe the stacks of mail they see there each year just before Christmas.

Elsewhere there's a city park where a 22-foot-tall statue of the jolly old man gazes down on the "little people of the world" to whom he is dedicated. Another Santa image sits atop a candy-striped water tower. The names of just about everything contribute to the aura of fantasy—Silver Bell Terrace, Donder Lane, Sled Run, Lake Rudolph, Lake Holly, Lake Noel, the Snowflake Drive-in, the Christmas Lake Village housing development, a newspaper called *Santa's Country.* Some town shops carry out the Christmas theme in their architecture, and Santa Claus Land opened in 1946 as the first theme park in the nation.

Recently Santa Claus Land was renamed **Holiday World,** but it still has all the attractions that endeared it to countless children—and adults—in the past. Santa's headquarters are there, of course, as are lots of toys; the animal farm where Santa's reindeer rest up for their arduous Christmas Eve journey; a variety of live musical, magical, and trained animal shows; a wax museum (the Hall of Famous Americans); antique toy and doll museums; a wave pool; a country music show; and a bevy of rides. If you dismiss all this as child's play, you should know that there are senior citizens from all over who make regular visits here.

The one-price admission, extremely reasonable by today's standards, entitles a guest to ride all rides and see all shows and attractions; children two and under are admitted free. In general, Holiday World opens at 10:00 A.M. daily mid-May to mid-August and on weekends in April, early May, late August, September, and October; it closes at 10:00 P.M. mid-June through mid-August and around dusk at other times. Holiday World may also be open on weekends from late November through the last weekend before Christmas. Because hours vary from year to year, it is best to request a schedule in advance. Contact Holiday World, P.O. Box 179, Santa Claus 47579; (812) 937–4401 or 1–800–467–2682. Santa Claus, the village, is located on State Road 245 in the north central part of the county.

Spencer County's second famous resident is immortalized in the pages of history books. When people think of Abraham Lincoln they usually think of the states of Kentucky and Illinois, but it was in Indiana that a young Abe went to school, worked the land, and grew to manhood. Abe's father, Thomas Lincoln, brought his small family here in 1816 and homesteaded 160 acres along the banks of Little Pigeon Creek. Indiana was a wilderness then, a forest of giant oaks, maples, and hickories where open views of even 200 yards were rare. Lincoln himself described it thus, in a poem he wrote many years after leaving the state.

> *When first my father settled here*
> *'Twas then the frontier line.*
> *The panther's scream filled the night with fear,*
> *And bears preyed on the swine.*

In 1818, when Abe was nine and his sister Sarah was eleven, their beloved mother died, and little more than a year later a lonely

Thomas married Sara Bush Johnston. A widow with three children, she raised Abe and Sarah as though they were her own, lavishing such love and affection on them that she forever tarnished the image of the wicked stepmother. She recognized the intimations of future greatness in young Abe and encouraged him to study, and Abe, on his part, loved her as few children love even their natural parents. When an adult Abe said, "All that I am, or hope to be, I owe to my angel Mother," he was speaking of his stepmother.

Lincoln left Indiana when he was twenty-one and moved to Illinois with his family, but his tenure in Spencer County is honored in a series of memorials. The ◆ **Lincoln Boyhood National Memorial** is next door to Lincoln State Park on State Road 162, just south of Lincoln City. Abe's biological mother, Nancy Hanks Lincoln, is buried at the former, and her grave and the reconstructed Lincoln cabin can be visited in this 200-acre park. A living-history farm that covers eighty acres of the Lincolns' original homestead is worked as Abe and his father once worked it and provides a fascinating, accurate insight into a way of life that shaped one of the our nation's greatest men.

At the handsome visitor center, you can view exhibits related to Lincoln's fourteen years in Indiana and see a twenty-seven-minute film about his life. You can also learn much about the human side of Lincoln, little-known facts that breathe life into the saintly image. Young Abe, for instance, loved to wrestle and was recognized as one of the area's best tusslers. His great physical strength earned him the nickname "young Hercules of Pigeon Creek," and he could hoist more weight and drive an ax deeper than any other man around. In 1828 his horizons widened greatly when he accompanied the son of the richest man in the community on a flatboat journey down the Ohio and Mississippi rivers to New Orleans. And one can only speculate how the course of history might have differed had Abe grown up in Kentucky, where slavery was tolerated. The national memorial is open 8:00 A.M. to 5:00 P.M. daily year-round, except major winter holidays; nominal admission fee. Costumed interpreters work the farm from mid-April through late October. Contact Lincoln Boyhood National Memorial, National Park Service, P.O. Box 1816, Lincoln City 47552; (812) 937–4541.

The adjacent **Lincoln State Park,** which covers nearly 1,800 acres, includes the grave of Lincoln's sister, who died in childbirth; the site of the Little Pigeon River Primitive Baptist Church, where the Lincoln family worshiped; and the site of the first school attended by Abe, who was eleven years old at the time. At 8:00 P.M. each night except Monday, from mid-June to late August, the story of Lincoln's life in Indiana is depicted in *Young Abe Lincoln,* a musical outdoor drama that's staged in the park's covered amphitheater. Performances of *Big River,* a Tony award–winning musical adapted from Mark Twain's *The Adventures of Huckleberry Finn,* alternate with *Young Abe Lincoln.* For details and reservations contact Young Abe Lincoln, P.O. Box 7–21, Lincoln City 47552; (800) 264–4223 or (812) 937–4493 in-season and 464–0029 off-season. You'll also find many opportunities here for outdoor recreation, as well as campsites and housekeeping cabins. Open daily year-round, during daylight hours; nominal vehicle admission fee is charged from spring through fall. Write Lincoln State Park, Box 216, Lincoln City 47552; (812) 937–4710.

On the banks of the Ohio River just west of Troy, the **Lincoln Ferry Landing State Wayside Park** on State Road 66 preserves another historical segment of Abe's life. Here, as an employee of a local farmer, sixteen-year-old Abe operated a ferry across the mouth of Anderson Creek, a tributary of the Ohio now called Anderson River. To increase his income Abe built himself a scow to carry passengers to Ohio River steamboats in midstream. His first experience with the legal profession came when he was hauled into a Kentucky court for ferrying passengers on the Ohio without a license (the Ohio River was considered part of Kentucky). Lincoln pleaded his own case, stating that he didn't believe the law applied to a ferryman who went only halfway across the river. Agreeing with him, the judge dismissed the case. Abe's fascination with the law began with that encounter.

Following State Road 66 west along the banks of the Ohio, you come to Rockport, where the **Rockport Inn** offers one of the most unusual lodging experiences in southern Indiana. This tiny hostelry, originally built as a private residence around 1855, contains just six bedrooms. No two bedrooms are alike, but each has air-conditioning and a private bath. Thoroughly renovated with painstaking care in recent years, the building retains as much of the original aura and design as the owners could achieve. Turn-of-the-century furnishings throughout contribute to the overall effect. Open year-round, the moderately priced inn serves meals on a rotating basis in its full-service restaurant. A continental breakfast is included in the room rates. Lunch is offered Tuesday through Saturday and dinner Wednesday through Saturday. There's also a Saturday brunch, but no meals at all are served on Sunday or Monday. Contact the Rockport Inn, 130 South Third Street, Rockport 47635; (812) 649–2664.

Also in Rockport is **Lincoln Pioneer Village.** Although all the log cabins are reconstructions, they reflect the lifestyle of Lincoln's boyhood years, and you can learn more interesting facts about our sixteenth president here. Situated at 222 South Third Street, the village is open 9:00 A.M. to 5:00 P.M. Tuesday through Sunday. Contact the Rockport Area Chamber of Commerce, 302 Main Street, P.O. Box 85, Rockport 47635; (812) 649–4626.

VANDERBURGH COUNTY

If architecture is your cup of tea, you'll want to tour two aesthetic treats in Evansville. The P.O. Box 1816, ◆ **John Augustus Reitz Home** at 224 Southeast First Street was erected in 1872 when Evansville was the hardwood capital of the country and Reitz was the "pioneer lumber king." Encircled by a black wrought-iron fence, the French Imperial house boasts three stories, seventeen rooms, ten fireplaces, and a display of Victorian-era opulence in the parquet floors, gilded bronze chandeliers, stained-glass windows, pier mirrors, gold-leaf cornices, and rare carved woods. Some of the first-floor ceilings are canvas, hand-painted in oil to match the original rugs. All heating units were turned on their sides and placed under the floor so that the radiators wouldn't show. The fireplaces were apparently for ornamentation only—they were never used. In the basement is a huge clothes dryer where clothes were hung on movable racks and dried by a gas heater beneath them.

The Reitz home sits in a 17-block historic district amid other massive homes built by wealthy owners who spent a considerable part of their fortunes trying to outdo the next fellow, but the home of the pioneer lumber king is the showplace of them all. Now a museum, it's open to the public from 1:00 to 4:00 P.M. Wednesday through Sunday, April through October. Visitors are taken on a half-hour tour, with the last tour beginning at 3:30 P.M.

Nominal admission fee. Special tours can be arranged by calling (812) 426–1871.

The **Old Courthouse** that dominates the Evansville cityscape, built between 1888 and 1891, is one of the grandest in the country. During its construction special excursion trains brought visitors from Louisville, St. Louis, and many other midwestern towns to admire what was then regarded as one of the most elegant buildings ever erected in the Midwest.

Its Indiana limestone face is encrusted with an unbelievable number of sculptures and stone carvings, some of heroic proportions, each intricately detailed—fourteen statues, national emblems, ornamental friezes, cherubs, innumerable garlands of flora indigenous to the area, and Indiana's state seal. Inside are marble floors and wainscots, oak woodwork, brass handrails, silver-plated hardware, domes, and an awesome rotunda.

Abandoned by the county government in 1969, the Old Courthouse now contains boutiques, art galleries, import shops, clothing stores, and a community repertory company. You'll find the magnificent old building at the corner of Fourth and Vine; it's open 8:00 A.M. to 5:00 P.M. Monday through Friday and 1:00 to 5:00 P.M. Saturday and Sunday. Guided tours are available by appointment. Contact the Old Courthouse Preservation Society, 201 Northwest Fourth Street, Room 114, Evansville 47708; (812) 423–3361.

At **Wesselman Park** you'll find 210 acres of primeval woodland. A virgin forest is extremely rare, but this one is particularly unusual because it lies entirely within the limits of a city and is of such high quality (most stands of woodland in or near cities have been adversely affected by pollution). A melting pot of northern and southern botanical species, ◆ **Wesselman Woods** is dominated by sweet gum trees. Spring here is bright with the blossoms of dogwood and redbud trees and with the wildflowers that are at their feet; autumn is a blaze of color. At the edge of the woods is a nature center where one-way glass provides a unique view of wildlife activity and a microphone brings sound and song indoors.

The woods, designated both a state nature preserve and a National Natural Landmark, make up approximately half of Wesselman Park; the remaining 200 acres offer typical recreational facilities, including a swimming pool. Along the park's northern boundary is a remnant stretch of the old **Wabash and Erie**

Canal, the longest ever built in this country. Only two boats ever traveled its entire 468-mile length from Evansville to Toledo, Ohio.

The park lies on the east side of Evansville at 551 North Boeke Road. Admission is free. The grounds are open daily year-round, from early morning until sunset. The nature center is open 8:30 A.M. to 5:00 P.M. Tuesday through Saturday and noon to 5:00 P.M. Sunday during summer months. Hours vary the rest of the year. Call (812) 479–0771.

Moundbuilder Indians, too, found this part of the country to their liking. Sometime around A.D. 1300, they built a village on the banks of the Ohio River southeast of Evansville and stayed there for about 200 years before moving on. The eleven mounds they abandoned in this spot constitute the largest and best-preserved group in the state. One, the central mound, covers more than four acres in area and measures 44 feet in height, making it one of the largest such structures in the eastern United States.

After years of archaeological excavations here, the 430-acre site was opened to the public as ◆ **Angel Mounds State Historic Site.** Visitors can view a simulated excavation site and many artifacts from the digs in a modern interpretive center, then walk the trails that lead among the mounds and reconstructed buildings of the Indian village. The memorial is located at 8215 Pollack Avenue, 7 miles southeast of downtown Evansville. Free admission; open 9:00 A.M. to 5:00 P.M. Tuesday through Saturday and 1:00 to 5:00 P.M. Sunday, mid-March through December; (812) 853–3956.

It seems to have become the thing to do in recent years for sports stars to enter the restaurant business and fill their eateries with sports memorabilia. Only in Indiana, however, will you find two such restaurants that include free-throw basketball courts in their decorating schemes. One is found at Larry Bird's Boston Connection in Terre Haute (see Vigo County below); for a professional basketball star, that's understandable. The other, however, is at **Mattinglys' 23,** whose half-owner, Evansville native Don Mattingly, is one of the best professional baseball players around. Mattingly, you see, like most Hoosier State youngsters, grew up wanting to be a basketball player, but his physical attributes and talents were more suited to baseball. Named for Mattingly's New York Yankees' uniform number, the restaurant reflects its owner's love for sports in general. There are, for example, a baseball legends room, a boxing ring with tables inside the ropes, a Hoosier room honoring local sports notables, a locker containing a Larry Bird Boston Celtics uniform, and a display that depicts the making of a Louisville Slugger bat (the Don Mattingly model). During the off-season Mattingly stops by three or four nights a week to visit with customers, sign autographs, and just generally help out. (Peeling potatoes, busing tables, tending bar, or making the occasional pizza from scratch are among his contributions.) It should be noted that the food, be it hamburger or filet mignon, is excellent, and the prices are moderate. Mattinglys' 23, located at 1700 Morgan Center Drive in Evansville, is open 11:00 A.M. to 10:00 P.M. Monday through Thursday and 11:00 A.M. to 10:30 P.M. Friday and Saturday. Reservations are recommended; call (812) 473–4323.

VIGO COUNTY

Larry Bird arrived in Terre Haute in 1975 a virtual unknown and left in 1979 a legend. During the four years he spent here as an Indiana State University student, he elevated ISU's basketball team from the ranks of the unknown to national fame by leading it through an undefeated season to the 1979 NCAA Championship Finals. Bird and the ISU Sycamores lost that final game to Michigan State, but Bird was named the 1978–79 College Player of the Year before moving on to a career in professional basketball with the Boston Celtics. There the honors continued. Bird was chosen the National Basketball Association's Rookie of the Year and later became the first forward in NBA history to win three Most Valuable Player Awards. He also led the Celtics to three world championships in the 1980s, and when he lifted one of those world championship trophies above his head and said, "This one's for Terre Haute!" he endeared himself to that city forever.

Given the special affection Bird and Terre Haute have for each other, it came as no surprise that Terre Haute was chosen as the home of **Larry Bird's Boston Connection,** a full-service hotel that could just as easily pass itself off as a basketball museum. Bird's many trophies and memorabilia from high school to the NBA as well as the Olympic Gold Medal Bird earned as part of the U.S.A.'s "Dream Team" in 1992, are prominently on display. A gift shop is stocked with Celtics souvenirs. All Celtics basketball games, as well as other sporting events, are shown on big-screen television in the Bird's Nest Sports Lounge. Guests dine beneath the Celtics championship banners that hang from the ceiling of the Boston Garden Family Restaurant. While waiting for such home-cooked Hoosier specialties as fried chicken, Swiss steak, and French Lick fries (named for Bird's hometown), guests can test their shooting skills in the dining room's glassed-in free-throw area—a green-and-white basketball is provided. Fans find the food as palatable as the atmosphere. The restaurant is open 6:30 A.M. to 9:00 P.M. Sunday through Thursday and 6:30 A.M. to 10:00 P.M. Friday and Saturday. Located at 555 South Third Street; (812) 235–3333 or 1–800–255–3399 in Indiana and 1–800–262–0033 outside Indiana. Those who have followed Larry Bird's career should have no trouble remembering the phone numbers—Bird has worn number 33 on every one of his uniforms from high school on.

Bibliophiles and intellectuals will find the **Cunningham Memorial Library** on the campus of Indiana State University of special interest. It houses what is said to be the world's largest collection of old and rare dictionaries—more than 12,000 volumes dating back to 1475 that represent the entire history of Western lexicography. Among them are more than 200 editions and issues of Samuel Johnson's *A Dictionary of the English Language*. Known as the **Cordell Collection,** it grew from an initial donation of 500 dictionaries by Warren Cordell, an ISU alumnus and executive with Nielsen's television-rating firm. The collection, located in the library's Rare Books and Special Collections section on the third floor, is open free of charge throughout the year. Hours vary; call (812) 237–2580 or 237–3773.

WARRICK COUNTY

Early in this century the family was the single most important thing in most people's lives. Three or more generations of families often lived together in the same house. People were born and died at home. The possibility of death was something confronted on an everyday basis, especially in rural America. Crops died, livestock died, people died.

When a family member died, he or she might lie in state at home for two or three days while a memorial wake and funeral took place. The tools of the local undertaker (originally a folklore term meaning "one who undertakes anything") were necessarily portable in those days, since he generally went to his customers rather than vice versa. All that changed in 1939, however, when a state law was passed that declared funerals could no longer be held at home.

Although that era no longer exists, it can be revisited at the **Simpson Mortuary Museum** in Newburgh. The Simpson family, which owns a modern-day funeral home just across the street from the museum, established the museum to preserve our ancestors' views of death—and life.

Among the interesting artifacts, most of which came from a local turn-of-the-century funeral home, is a summer cooling board. Pans of ice were placed beneath the perforated board to cool the deceased throughout a wake. A rare Rockaway Buggy was the typical mode of transportation for early-twentieth-century undertakers. When a person died away from his residence, he was discreetly transported home in a wicker body basket like the one at the museum.

The museum, housed in a small brick building approximately two hundred years old, may be seen free of charge by appointment. Contact Simpson Funeral Home, 510 West Jennings Street, Newburgh 47630; (812) 853–8314. When phoning, call on weekdays before noon.

First settled in 1803, Newburgh perches picturesquely on the banks of Ohio River. The town contains some lovely restored homes, and a 4-square-block section in the downtown area is on the National Register of Historic Places. For additional information contact **Historic Newburgh, Inc.,** 100 State Street, P.O. Box 543, Newburgh 47629; (812) 853–2815. Historic Newburgh's office is open 10:00 A.M. to 4:00 P.M. Monday through Friday and noon to 4:00 P.M. Saturday.

GENERAL INDEX

Entries for Museums and Nature Preserves appear only in the special indexes

A

Abbott's Candy Shop, 107
Adams County, 34–36
Adam's Rib, 2
Alamo, 71
Allen County, 36–39
Alpine Acres, 13–15
Alpine Slide, 116
Amish Acres, 44
Amishville, U.S.A., 34
Anderson University, 13
Angel Mounds State Historic Site, 165
Angelo Bernacchi Green-houses, 67
Antique Farm Power Show, 79
Appleseed Park, Johnny, 36
Archives of Traditional Music, 140
Arnold's Candy Store, 56
Auction Restaurant, 53
Ault Stables, 51

B

Back 40 Junction Restaurant, 35–36
Ball/Kraft collection of ancient glass, 41–42
Ball State University, 41
Barker Civic Center, 67–68
Barn House,147–48
Barnum, P. T., 58
Bartholomew County, 82-85
Bean Blossom Bluegrass Festival, 112

Bear's Place, 136
Beatty, Clyde, 55
Beaver Bend, bluffs of, 133–34
Bell's Ford Bridge, 99
Best of Indiana, The, 20
Big Ben, 48
Big River, 162
Billie Creek Bridge, 150
Billie Creek Village, 150
Bird, Larry, 142, 166–67
Black Horse Troop, 69–70
Blue River, 120
Bluespring Caverns, 130
Bodine State Fish Hatchery, Richard Clay, 78
Boggstown Inn & Cabaret, 30-31
Boone County, 2-3
Boone County Courthouse, 2
Borders, Bruce, 113–14
Bridgeton Bridge, 148
Bronson Cave, 131
Brouillet French House, 127
Brown County, 110–18
Brown County Art Gallery, 110–11
Brown County Art Guild, 110
Brown County Democrat, 117
Brown County Playhouse, 111–12
Brown County Sorghum Mill, 115
Brown County State Park, 114
Brown County Winter Fest, 116

MUSEUMS

NATURE PRESERVES

ACKNOWLEDGEMENTS

If I were to personally thank each person who has contributed in some way to the writing of this book, the list would be longer than the contents of the book itself. I talked to many people during my travels throughout Indiana. They were, without exception, warm, gracious, and kind. We met strangers and parted as friends. I am grateful to each and every one of them.

UNITED STATES TRAVEL

Off the Beaten Path™ Series

These are some fine guides from our *Off the Beaten Path* series designed for the traveler who enjoys the special and unusual. Each book is by an author who knows the state well, did extensive research, and personally visited many of the places, often more than once. Please check your local bookstore for fine Globe Pequot Press titles, which include:

Alabama, $10.95	Missouri, $10.95
Arkansas, $10.95	Montana, $10.95
Colorado, $10.95	New Hampshire, $10.95
Connecticut, $10.95	New Jersey, $10.95
Florida, $10.95	New Mexico, $10.95
Georgia, $10.95	New York, $10.95
Hawaii, $12.95	Northern California, $10.95
Idaho, $10.95	North Carolina, $10.95
Illinois, $10.95	Ohio, $10.95
Iowa, $10.95	Oregon, $10.95
Indiana, $10.95	Pennsylvania, $10.95
Kansas, $10.95	Southern California, $10.95
Kentucky, $10.95	Tennessee, $10.95
Louisiana, $10.95	Texas, $10.95
Maine, $10.95	Vermont, $10.95
Maryland, $10.95	Virginia, $10.95
Massachusetts, $10.95	Washington, $10.95
Michigan, $10.95	West Virginia, $10.95
Minnesota, $10.95	Wisconsin, $10.95

To order any of these titles with MASTERCARD or VISA, call toll-free (800) 243-0495; or fax us at (800) 820-2329 (24 hours a day). Free shipping for orders of three or more books. Shipping charge of $3.00 per book for one or two books ordered. Connecticut residents add sales tax. Ask for your free catalogue of Globe Pequot's quality books on recreation, travel, nature, gardening, cooking, crafts, and more. Prices and availability subject to change.